Benziger

Eucharist

We Give Thanks and Praise

Do this in memory of me.
from Luke 22:19

General Editors

Sister Catherine Dooley, O.P.
Monsignor Thomas McDade, Ed.D.

The Ad Hoc Committee to Oversee the Use of the Catechism, United States Conference of Catholic Bishops, has found this catechetical text, copyright © 2006, to be in conformity, as supplemental catechetical material, with the *Catechism of the Catholic Church.*

Acknowledgments

Consultants: James Gaffney, Enrico Hernandez, Monica Hughes, David Michael Thomas

Contributors: Jane Ayer, Sylvia DeVillers, Janie Gustafson, Marianne Lenihan, Joanne McPortland, Margaret Savitskas, Rita Burns-Senseman

Music: Gary Daigle

Spanish: José Segovia, María Elena Carrión

Production: Monotype Productions

Nihil Obstat: Sister Karen Wilhelmy, CSJ, Censor Deputatus

Imprimatur: † Roger Cardinal Mahony, Archbishop of Los Angeles, September 2005

The nihil obstat and imprimatur are official declarations that the work contains nothing contrary to Faith and Morals. It is not implied, thereby, that those who have granted the nihil obstat and imprimatur agree with the contents, statements, or opinions expressed.

Photo Credits: 3: (tr) Gene Plaisted, OSC / The Crosiers, (tcr) Creatas / PunchStock, (cr) Giulio Broglio / AP Wide World Photos, (br) Creatas / PunchStock, (bl) Bill and Peggy Wittman ; 5: (br) Amos Morgan / Getty Images; 8: (l) Bill and Peggy Wittman; 9: (tl) Bill and Peggy Wittman, (tr) Bill and Peggy Wittman; 10: (tl) Bill and Peggy Wittman, (tr) Alan Oddie / Photo Edit, (br) Tony Freeman / Photo Edit, (bl) Bill and Peggy Wittman; 11: (bkgd) PhotoLink / Getty Images; 16: Gene Plaisted, OSC / The Crosiers; 17: (t) Gene Plaisted, OSC / The Crosiers; 18: (l) Creatas / PunchStock, (r) Creatas / PunchStock; 19: (b) Creatas / PunchStock; 21: SW Productions / Getty Images; 24: (b) Bill and Peggy Wittman; 25: Gene Plaisted, OSC / The Crosiers; 26: (l) David Toase / Getty Images, (tr) PhotoDisc / PunchStock, (bl) Skip Nail / Getty Images; 27: (bkgd) Keith Brofsky/Getty Images; 28: Ken Cavanagh / McGraw-Hill; 29: Digital Vision / PunchStock; 32: (b) Gene Plaisted, OSC / The Crosiers; 33: (tl) Bill and Peggy Wittman; 34: (t) Giulio Broglio / AP Wide World Photos; 35: (bkgd) Brand X Pictures / PunchStock; 37: (b) Digital Vision / PunchStock; 40: (b) Tony Freeman / Photo Edit; 43: (bkgd) Medioimages / PunchStock; 48: (b) Bill and Peggy Wittman; 49: (l) Bill and Peggy Wittman, (r) CLEO PHOTOGRAPHY / Photo Edit; 51: (bkgd) Royalty-free / Corbis, (b) Brand X Pictures / Getty Images; 53: (r) Doug Menuez / Getty Images, (br) John A. Rizzo / Getty Images, (br) Image100 / PunchStock; 56: (l) Bill & Peggy Wittman, (r) Image100 / PunchStock; 57: (l) Royalty-free / Corbis, (r) Greg Ceo / Getty Images; 59: (bkgd) Brand X / Getty Images; 61: Gene Plaisted, OSC / The Crosiers; 62-063: (c) Digital Vision / PunchStock; 63: (b) Gene Plaisted, OSC / The Crosiers, (t) Gene Plaisted, OSC / The Crosiers; 64: (l) Bill and Peggy Wittman; 65: (t) Bill and Peggy Wittman, (b) Bill and Peggy Wittman; 66: (t) Creatas / PunchStock; 67: Rob Lewine / Corbis; 72: (br) Gabe Palmer / Corbis; 75: (r) Bill and Peggy Wittman; 77:(br) Creatas / PunchStock; 83: (br) Bill and Peggy Wittman; 88: (tl) Brand X Pictures / PunchStock, (br) Brand X Pictures / PunchStock.

Illustration Credits: 6: (b) Robin Dewitt; 7: Robin Dewitt; 13: (b) Gershom Griffith; 14-15: (b) Frank Mayo; 22-23: (b) Jim Conaway; 30-31: Lane Gregory; 38-39: (b) Pat Paris; 45: (b) Diana Magnuson; 46: (b) Frank Mayo; 47: (b) Frank Mayo; 54-55: (b) Jim Conaway; 82: (b) Chris Dyrud.

A

*The **McGraw-Hill** Companies*

Published by Macmillan/McGraw-Hill, of McGraw-Hill Education, a division of The McGraw-Hill Companies, Inc., Two Penn Plaza, New York, New York 10121.

Send all inquiries to:
Benziger
Two Penn Plaza, 21st Floor
New York, New York 10121

ISBN 0-02-260162-7

Printed in the United States of America

1 2 3 4 5 6 7 8 9 006/055 09 08 07 06 05

Table of Contents

Welcome!

This is a special time for you and your family. You are taking one more step on your journey with Jesus.

This book will help you as you prepare to receive Holy Communion for the first time. You will learn that taking part in the Eucharist means much more than knowing correct words and actions. Eucharist means having a heart full of praise and thanks to God. Eucharist means walking with Jesus every day, and it means living in the Holy Spirit as you try to love and serve others.

Many people in your parish will be praying for you as you prepare for Holy Communion. This is a great celebration for the whole parish.

May God bless you and keep you close.

Belonging

For through faith you are all children of God.
Galatians 3:26

Mike's New Family

Mike had always known his chances weren't good. He had ongoing medical problems and difficulty walking. Besides, he wasn't a cute little kid anymore. People preferred to adopt a baby or a young child, not a ten-year old.

Then one day Mike met Emily and Joe Brown. They seemed to like him from the very beginning. Eventually, they asked him to be their son. Mike was excited, but also afraid. Would they change their minds if he got ill again?

Mike did get sick again, but Emily and Joe did not feel any differently about him. "We love you," they told him. "And that love will last forever."

Through Emily and Joe, Mike learned about God's love for him. When they spoke to Mike about becoming a member of the Catholic Church, he really got excited. Emily and Joe explained that this would happen at the Easter Vigil. Before then, he would need to prepare well for his initiation into the Church.

- **What difference did Emily and Joe's love make in Mike's life?**
- **Think about someone whose love has made a difference in your life. Pray to God thanking him for the gift of this person.**

A New Beginning

Word of God

I have called you by name;
you are mine.

Isaiah 43:1

It was finally time for the Easter Vigil. Mike had spent more than a year studying, praying, and thinking about the Catholic faith. There had been time for him to pray with the parish community. Tonight, he would become a full member of the Catholic Church through the Sacraments of Baptism, Confirmation, and Eucharist.

Mike listened carefully to the Gospel reading about Mary Magdalene and the other women finding Jesus' empty tomb on Easter. Two men in dazzling garments appeared and spoke to the women.

"Why do you seek the living one among the dead? He is not here, but he has been raised. Remember what he said to you while he was still in Galilee, that the Son of Man must be handed over to sinners and be crucified, and rise on the third day."

(Luke 24:5–7)

After the Gospel, Father Bill explained that Jesus' death, Resurrection, and Ascension (the Paschal Mystery) is a very important belief of the Catholic faith. Easter is a time for all followers of Christ to affirm their belief in the Resurrection.

"Yes", Mike prayed. "I do believe in the Risen Christ."

After the homily, Father Bill and those to be baptized and their godparents gathered around the baptismal font. After Mike's profession of faith, the priest baptized him by pouring water three times on his head and saying, "I baptize you in the name of the Father, and of the Son, and of the Holy Spirit."

The ceremony continued when Father Bill anointed Mike's head with sacred chrism and confirmed him. Later in the Mass, Mike would receive the Eucharist for the first time. This would complete his initiation into the Church. It would begin his new life of grace and make him an heir to God's kingdom.

Let's Talk

- Why is the Paschal Mystery of Jesus such an important belief?
- What did Mike do to become a member of the Church?
- How do you experience dying and rising in your life?

We Celebrate

This is our faith. This is the faith of the Church. We are proud to profess it, in Christ Jesus our Lord. Amen.

Rite of Baptism, #96

Sacraments of Initiation

Catholics have three special signs of belonging to God's family. These signs are called the **Sacraments of Christian Initiation**. An initiation is a process, or series of steps, needed to join a group. Through Christian Initiation, you become a member of the Church. The three Sacraments of Christian Initiation are **Baptism, Confirmation,** and **Eucharist**.

A **sacrament** is a special sign of God's love that Jesus gave to his followers. Each sacrament uses visible signs, or symbols, from daily life that show what is spiritually happening within you. Each sacrament strengthens your relationship with God and with the members of the Church family. Each sacrament helps you be more loving.

The visible signs of Baptism remind you about the way followers of Jesus are to live and act. When the water, a sign of new life, is poured at Baptism, sin is taken away and you are called to turn away from sin throughout your life. The oil, a sign of the gift of the Holy Spirit, is a reminder to be strong in faith. The white garment reminds you to put on the mind and heart of Jesus, to follow his example. The lit candle is a reminder to bring God's light to the world.

Baptism is the first sacrament you celebrate. Baptism gives you new life in Christ, takes away **original sin** and all sins, and makes you a member of the Body of Christ, the Church.

Confirmation completes Baptism. In this sacrament, the Holy Spirit seals, or confirms, your relationship with Christ and the Church. At Confirmation, the bishop or his representative makes the Sign of the Cross on your forehead with sacred chrism. He says, "Be sealed with the Gift of the Holy Spirit." The Holy Spirit helps you live your Baptism and act as a loving member of God's family.

At Eucharist, you are given the Body and Blood of Christ under the appearance of bread and wine. With these three sacraments, your Christian initiation is complete. You are a full member of the Catholic Church.

This We Believe

Sacraments of Christian Initiation welcome us to full membership in the Church. They give us a share in God's own life and love.

Look at the photos on these pages and review the meaning of the signs of Baptism. **Write a caption for each picture.**

1. ______________________________
2. ______________________________
3. ______________________________

Living Your Baptism

The signs of Baptism will help you to live out the sacrament. For each sign, write or draw a picture of what you will do this week to show that you are a child of God.

What I Will Do

1 Turn away from sin.

2 Be strong in faith.

3 Follow Jesus.

4 Bring light to others.

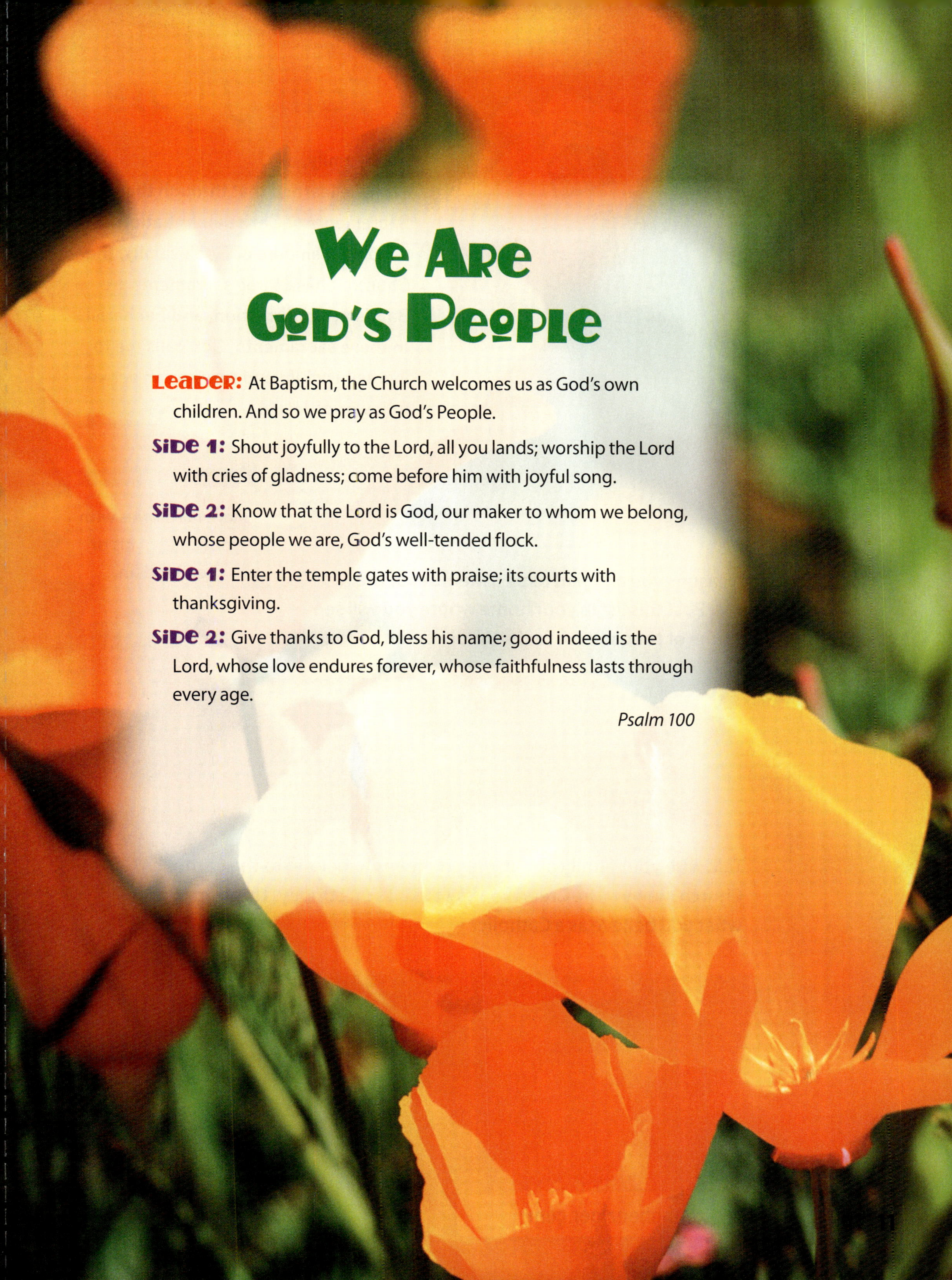

We Are God's People

Leader: At Baptism, the Church welcomes us as God's own children. And so we pray as God's People.

Side 1: Shout joyfully to the Lord, all you lands; worship the Lord with cries of gladness; come before him with joyful song.

Side 2: Know that the Lord is God, our maker to whom we belong, whose people we are, God's well-tended flock.

Side 1: Enter the temple gates with praise; its courts with thanksgiving.

Side 2: Give thanks to God, bless his name; good indeed is the Lord, whose love endures forever, whose faithfulness lasts through every age.

Psalm 100

Family Note

Dear Family,

I have learned that through the Sacraments of Christian Initiation we become members of God's family, the Church. These three sacraments are Baptism, Confirmation, and Eucharist. In these sacraments, God calls me to live as his child and serve as an active follower of Jesus.

Family Chat

Share memories with your child of his or her Baptism.

ON YOUR OWN

Make a list of reasons you are glad to be a member of the Catholic Church. Post this list in your home where you will see it during your time of preparation for First Holy Communion.

WITH YOUR FAMILY

Talk with your family about what it means to belong to the Catholic Church. Review the Creed you say at Mass on Sunday. This sums up what you believe as a Catholic.

Go Online! www.mhbenziger.com

Gathering

We, though many, are one body.
1 Corinthians 10:17

A Family Celebration

Instead of eating Thanksgiving dinner at home, Maria's family decided to eat at a restaurant. At first, Maria didn't know what to think. Being in a large room with strangers at other tables did not seem like a normal Thanksgiving at all.

When the waiter brought the food, however, Maria's feelings began to change. There were no menus as in a regular restaurant. Instead, the same meal was served to everyone. Also, the food didn't arrive already served on each plate. The waiter brought bowls of food and placed them on the table for everyone to share.

"It's called 'family style,'" Maria's mother explained.

Before long, Maria forgot where she was and simply enjoyed eating and talking as a family. She ended up having a great time. It really was a good way to have a family celebration.

- **Think about a time when your family got together to celebrate. Where did you eat? Who was there? What food was served?**
- **What is needed for a good family celebration?**

Gathering as Christians

Word of God

Now you are Christ's Body, and individually parts of it.

1 Corinthians 12:27

Jesus liked to gather together with friends for a meal. He ate at the home of Lazarus, and Lazarus' two sisters, Martha and Mary. One time, Jesus ate at the home of a sinner named Zacchaeus. At other times, he ate with religious leaders, tax collectors, and his disciples. At these meals, Jesus shared with others and talked about God's love and what it means to live as God's People.

After Jesus ascended to heaven, his followers continued to come together to pray and eat. During the meal, they talked about Jesus and what he had said and done. They talked about ways they could help others. They began to call themselves **Christians**, a name that means "followers of Christ." They felt like members of one family.

Communal Life

Listen to what Scripture tells us about the first Christians and their gatherings.

> "They devoted themselves to the teaching of the apostles and to the communal life, to the breaking of the bread and to the prayers. Awe came upon everyone, and many wonders and signs were done through the apostles. All who believed were together and had all things in common; they would sell their property and possessions and divide them among all according to each one's need. Every day they devoted themselves to meeting together in the temple area and to breaking bread in their homes. They ate their meals with exultation and sincerity of heart, praising God and enjoying favor with all the people."
>
> *Acts 2:42–47*

Let's Talk

- What did the first Christians do when they gathered together?
- How did they act as a family to each other?
- When do you gather with your Church family? What do you do together?
- How does your parish look out for those in need as the early Christians did?

Christians Today

This We Believe

When we gather to celebrate the Eucharist, we are one Church. We believe that Jesus remains with us in the sacraments.

Every Sunday **Catholics** gather together as the early Christians did to celebrate the Resurrection of Jesus. Those assembled remember Jesus, pray together, and take part in a special meal called the **Eucharist**. The Eucharist is also called the Mass and is led by a validly ordained Catholic priest. The Eucharist is at the heart of the life of the Church.

At the beginning of Mass, there an Introductory Rite. You stand and sing a song together while the priest and ministers walk in **procession** to the altar.

The priest says, "In the name of the Father and of the Son, and of the Holy Spirit."

You answer, "Amen."

These words say you believe that the Blessed Trinity—God the Father, God the Son, and God the Holy Spirit—is present with the people at Mass. The mystery of the Holy Trinity is the central mystery of our Christian faith and life.

After making the Sign of the Cross, the priest greets the people, saying "The Lord be with you." You respond with the rest of the people, "And also with you."

During the penitential rite, you praise God and thank him for his **mercy**, or forgiving love. You pray, "Lord have mercy. Christ have mercy. Lord have mercy."

Then you sing or pray the prayer, "Glory to God." This is an ancient hymn of praise which begins with the words of the angels at the birth of Jesus.

You gather at Mass to praise and thank God. Think about all that God has given you.

Name three things for which you are thankful.

1 ______________________________

 ______________________________

 ______________________________

Catholic Practices

The priest and ministers walk in procession into the church. The entrance procession joins people together into a community.

We Follow Jesus

The early Christians gathered together to remember Jesus. They prayed together and praised God. They were like family to one another. They helped those in need.

Work with a partner. Discuss the following questions:

1. When do you and your parish family gather together to remember Jesus?
2. How are members of the parish like family to one another?
3. How do members of your parish help those in need?

With your partner, make a poster that shows your answer to one of the questions. Give your poster a title.

We Give God Glory

Leader: Every time we gather as the Body of Christ, we give God glory. We can give God glory and praise right now as we pray:

All (Sing or Say): Glory and praise to our God.

Side 1: Lord God, heavenly King, almighty God and Father, we worship you.

Side 2: We give you thanks, we praise you for your glory.

All (Sing or Say): Glory and praise to our God.

Side 1: Lord Jesus Christ, only Son of the Father, Lord God, Lamb of God, you take away the sin of the world: have mercy on us.

Side 2: You are seated at the right hand of the Father: receive our prayer.

All (Sing or Say): Glory and praise to our God.

Side 1: For you alone are the Holy One, you alone are the Lord, you alone are the Most High, Jesus Christ.

Side 2: With the Holy Spirit, in the glory of God the Father. Amen.

All (Sing or Say): Glory and praise to our God.

Family Note

Dear Family,

I have learned that the first followers of Jesus were like a family. They prayed together, shared with one another, and helped the needy. You can help me prepare for Holy Communion by telling me how the Eucharist brings you closer to God and other Church members.

Family Chat

Share the reasons each person in the family has for going to Mass.

ON YOUR OWN

Pray for the other people in your Communion class. Ask God to help everyone act as a loving member of the Body of Christ.

WITH YOUR FAMILY

The next time you eat together as a family, talk about ways to show you are part of the parish family. Choose a parish activity you can do together.

 Go Online! www.mhbenziger.com

Listening

Blessed are those who hear the word of God and observe it.

Luke 11:28

Stories

Think of a time someone told you a story. Perhaps it was at a family gathering when someone told a story of long ago. Perhaps it was with a group of friends when funny stories were being told. Perhaps it was at school when someone told an interesting story in class. You probably listened carefully to the story. In listening, you showed your respect for the person telling the story. In listening to the story, you might even have learned something.

- What is a favorite story that someone told you?
- What did you learn from listening to the story?

Listen to Jesus

Word of God

Oh, that today you would hear his voice:
Do not harden your hearts.

Psalm 95:8

Jesus used stories to teach people about God's love. People who were eager to do God's will listened to his stories. One day, he told the story about the sower, a person who plants seeds.

> "A sower went out to sow. And as he sowed, some seed fell on the path, and birds came and ate it up. Some fell on rocky ground, where it had little soil. It sprang up at once because the soil was not deep, and when the sun rose it was scorched, and it withered for lack of roots. Some seed fell among thorns, and the thorns grew up and choked it. But some seed fell on rich soil, and produced fruit, a hundred or sixty or thirtyfold. Whoever has ears ought to hear."
>
> *Matthew 13:3–9*

Jesus Explains

Those listening to Jesus did not fully understand the story of the sower. Jesus explained what it meant.

> "The seed sown on the path is the one who hears the word of the kingdom without understanding it, and the evil one comes and steals away what was sown in his heart. The seed sown on rocky ground is the one who hears the word and receives it at once with joy. But he has no root and lasts only for a time. When some tribulation or persecution comes because of the word, he immediately falls away. The seed sown among thorns is the one who hears the word. But then worldly anxiety and the lure of riches choke the word and it bears no fruit. But the seed sown on rich soil is the one who hears the word and understands it, who indeed bears fruit and yields a hundred or sixty or thirtyfold."
>
> *Matthew 13:19–23*

Let's Talk

- In Jesus' story, what happened to the seeds the farmer scattered?
- How did Jesus explain the story?
- What did you learn from Jesus' story?
- What kind of ground do you want to be?

God's Word

Every week you hear God's Word when you go to Mass. God speaks to you and to all the people assembled. This time of listening to God's Word is called the **Liturgy of the Word**. It comes after the Introductory Rites of the Mass.

After you sit and prepare to listen, the lector reads the first reading. This is usually a story about the people of God who lived many years before Jesus. During Easter time the reading is from the Acts of the Apostles. At the end of this reading, the lector says, "The Word of the Lord." You answer, "Thanks be to God."

Everyone sings a song or psalm from Scripture called the Responsorial Psalm. A song leader or cantor leads the people in singing.

You listen to a second reading by the lector. This reading is taken from the New Testament of the Bible. It is a story about the first Christians. At the end of this reading, the lector again says, "The Word of the Lord." You answer as before, "Thanks be to God."

You stand and sing "Alleluia" at the Gospel Acclamation. Then you listen to the priest or deacon proclaim the **Gospel**. The word Gospel means "Good News." The Gospel reading tells about the wonderful things Jesus

Catholic Practices

The Creed prayed at Mass is called the Nicene Creed.

did and his message for all people. At the end of the Gospel, the priest or deacon says, "The Gospel of the Lord." You say, "Praise to you, Lord Jesus Christ."

The priest explains the Word of God and encourages you to follow it. This talk is called the **homily**. After the homily, you stand and pray the **Nicene Creed**. The Creed states the beliefs of the people of God in the Blessed Trinity—God the Father, God the Son, and God the Holy Spirit.

With the people assembled, you pray the Prayer of the Faithful. You ask God's help for everyone in need. One of the responses to these prayers is "Lord, hear our prayer."

Make an instruction booklet for the second graders who are preparing for First Communion.
Explain each part of the Mass in words the second graders will understand.

Parish Connection

Talk to a parish lector. Ask how he or she feels about proclaiming God's Word at Mass.

Acting on God's Word

Jesus said, "This is my commandment: love one another as I love you."

John 15:12

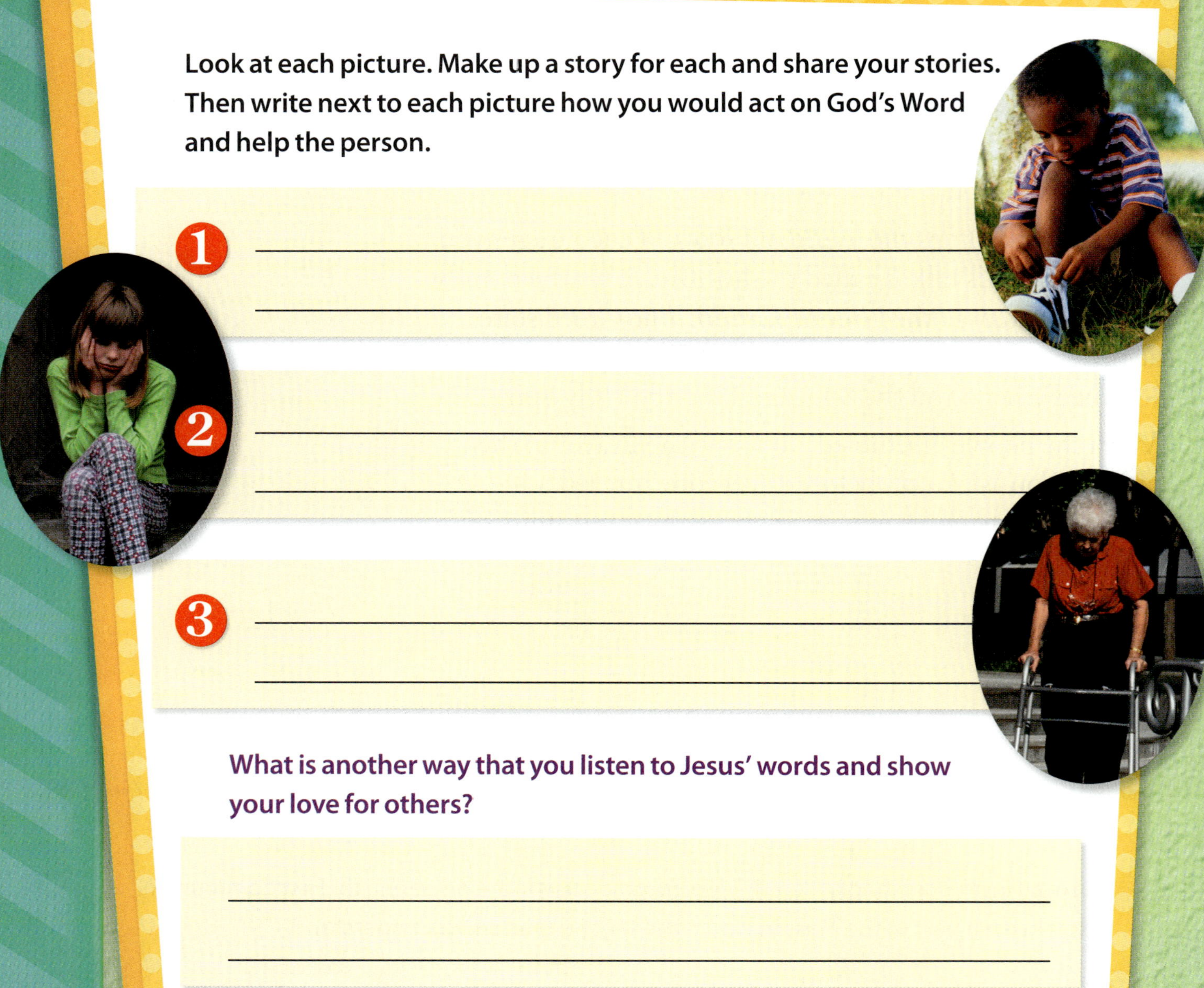

Look at each picture. Make up a story for each and share your stories. Then write next to each picture how you would act on God's Word and help the person.

1 ______________________________

____

2 ______________________________

____

3 ______________________________

____

What is another way that you listen to Jesus' words and show your love for others?

____

____

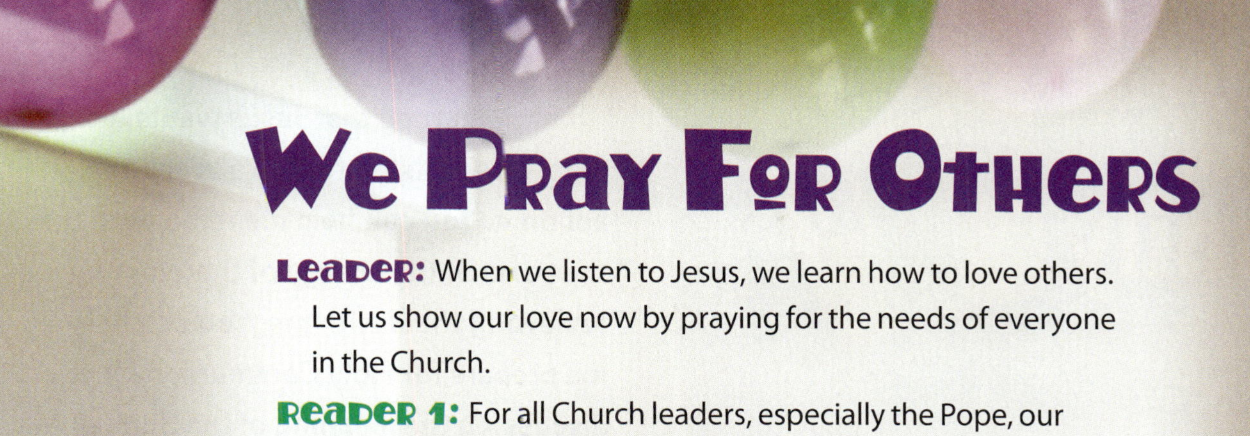

We Pray For Others

Leader: When we listen to Jesus, we learn how to love others. Let us show our love now by praying for the needs of everyone in the Church.

Reader 1: For all Church leaders, especially the Pope, our Bishop, and our Pastor, we pray to the Lord.

All: Lord, hear our prayer.

Reader 2: For all people who teach us about Jesus, we pray to the Lord.

All: Lord, hear our prayer.

Reader 3: For everyone in our parish, we pray to the Lord.

All: Lord, hear our prayer.

Reader 4: For people who are poor and needy, we pray to the Lord.

All: Lord, hear our prayer.

Reader 5: For all those preparing for First Communion and for their families, we pray to the Lord.

All: Lord, hear our prayer.

Leader: O God, we love to listen to your Word. Help us act on it every day. We make this prayer in Jesus' name.

All: Amen.

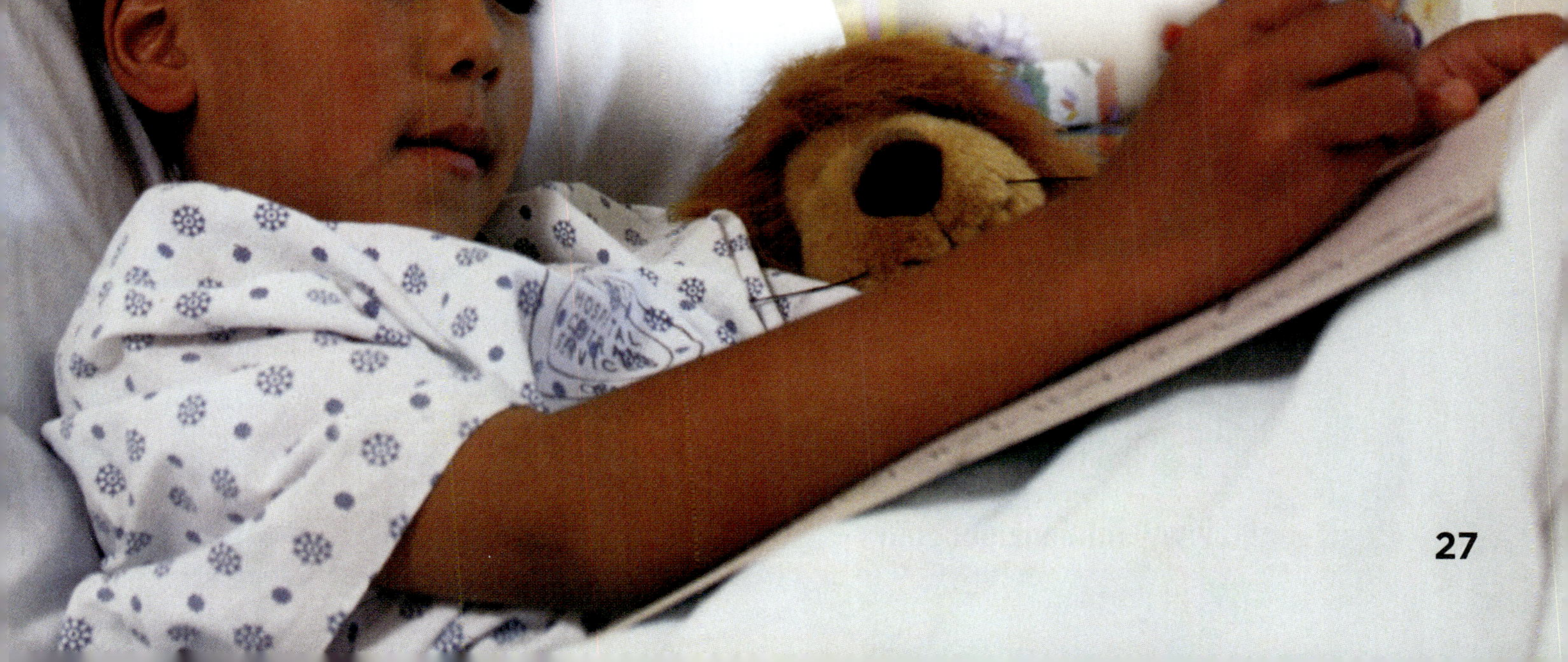

Family Note

Dear Family,

I have learned that Jesus wants his followers to listen to God's Word and act on it. You can help me remember the parts of the Liturgy of the Word by reviewing them with me. You can help me prepare for Holy Communion by discussing the meaning of the Sunday Gospel reading.

Family Chat

Talk about the message of Jesus and why it is Good News.

ON YOUR OWN

Make a bookmark that reminds you to listen to God's Word. Put the bookmark in a book you are reading now. Use these words:

Blessed are those who hear the word of God and observe it.

(Luke 11:28)

WITH YOUR FAMILY

Find out what the Gospel reading for this Sunday will be. Discuss its message. Write a sentence or draw a picture about what God's Word says to you.

Go Online! www.mhbenziger.com

Giving Thanks And Praise

Sing praise to the Lord, you faithful.
Psalm 30:5

Gifts

Kelly dreaded going back to school after Christmas break. Some of her classmates had great stories to tell about places they had been. Others boasted about the presents they had received.

Kelly knew her family couldn't afford such trips or expensive gifts. But it was still hard for her to be around students who seemed to have so much.

Kelly's mom knew she was feeling down. As she gave Kelly a hug, she said, "Remember, we're well off in our own way. We've got one another, we're healthy, and we have many gifts from God. And what I enjoy most is that a lot of love and laughter fills this house."

Kelly smiled as she thought about her mom's words. She did have many real gifts that couldn't be bought, lost, stolen, or broken. And they were the best gifts of all.

- What gifts do you have that cannot be bought, lost, stolen, or broken?
- Why do you think God gave you these gifts?

All Good Gifts

Word of God

If you know how to give good gifts to your children, how much more will your heavenly Father give good things to those who ask him.

Matthew 7:11

God has given you many gifts, including your life, your family, and all of creation. Everything we have, including God's love, is God's gift to us. God truly loves you and will always take care of you. You were made to be with God. One day Jesus explained to his disciples how great the Father's love really is.

"Therefore I tell you, do not worry about your life, what you will eat or drink, or about your body, what you will wear. Is not life more than food and the body more than clothing? Look at the birds in the sky; they do not sow or reap, they gather nothing into barns, yet your heavenly Father feeds them. Are not you more important than they? Can any of you by worrying add a single moment to your life-span? Why are you anxious about clothes?"

"Learn from the way the wild flowers grow. They do not work or spin. But I tell you that not even Solomon in all his splendor was clothed like one of them. If God so clothes the grass of the field, which grows today and is thrown into the oven tomorrow, will he not much more provide for you, O you of little faith? So do not worry and say, 'What are we to eat?' or 'What are we to drink?' or 'What are we to wear?' All these things the pagans seek. Your heavenly Father knows that you need them all. But seek first the kingdom [of God] and his righteousness, and all these things will be given you besides."

Matthew 6:25–33

Let's Talk

- What are some things you worry about?
- What is the message of Jesus about our worries?
- How has God taken care of you?

Thanking God

At every Eucharist, we remember the gift of creation and all other gifts God the Father has given us. The word *Eucharist* means "thanks and praise." **Thanks** means to be grateful for all the gifts God has given us. **Praise** means to give God glory for being so loving and generous.

The second part of Mass is called the **Liturgy of the Eucharist**. At the presentation of the gifts, bread and wine are brought to the altar. During this time in the Liturgy, the Church thanks God for his abundant gifts. The priest prepares the gift of bread on the altar. He says,

"Blessed are you, Lord, God of all creation. Through your goodness we have this bread to offer, which Earth has given and human hands have made. It will become for us the bread of life."

You respond, "Blessed be God forever."

After a similar prayer over the wine, the **Eucharistic Prayer** begins. It is the Church's great prayer of thanksgiving. The priest says, "Let us give thanks to the Lord, our God." You say, "It is right to give him thanks and praise." The Eucharistic Prayer is the prayer of the whole Church. It is the prayer of the assembly. It is your prayer, too. In it, you thank God for the gift of his Son, Jesus. You also thank God for many other special gifts:

We Celebrate

All: May the Lord accept the sacrifice at your hands for the praise and glory of his name, for our good, and the good of all his Church.

This We Believe

Jesus is true God and true man. For this reason he is the mediator between God and humankind.

- your own life and everything that helps you be happy
- all members of your parish and of the world Church
- church members who have died

The priest offers the gifts of our lives through the sacrifice of Christ's Passion which is re-presented at the Mass. He prays that everyone may be made one by the Holy Spirit. Together, we praise God and give him thanks.

Identify a gift for which you are particularly thankful to God.

Write a prayer of thanks to God.

____

____

____

____

____

Showing Thanks

Catholic Practices

The bread used at Mass has no yeast in it. The flat bread, made from wheat, is usually shaped into circles called hosts. The wine used is made from grapes.

Pope John Paul II said, "Christ's riches are for every individual and are everybody's property." You are rich because God the Father has given you many spiritual gifts. One way to thank God for these gifts is to use them in good ways and to share them with others, as his son Jesus did.

Here are some spiritual gifts God gives you. **Show how you can thank God for each gift by matching each gift with an appropriate action.**

1	**Faith**	______ Offer to help.
2	**Friendship**	______ Pray.
3	**Compassion**	______ Apologize.
4	**Gratitude**	______ Forgive someone.
5	**Self-control**	______ Say "thank you."
6	**Hope**	______ Show courage.
7	**Peace**	______ Trust God.
8	**Forgiveness**	______ Be patient.
9	**Strength**	______ Listen to a lonely person.

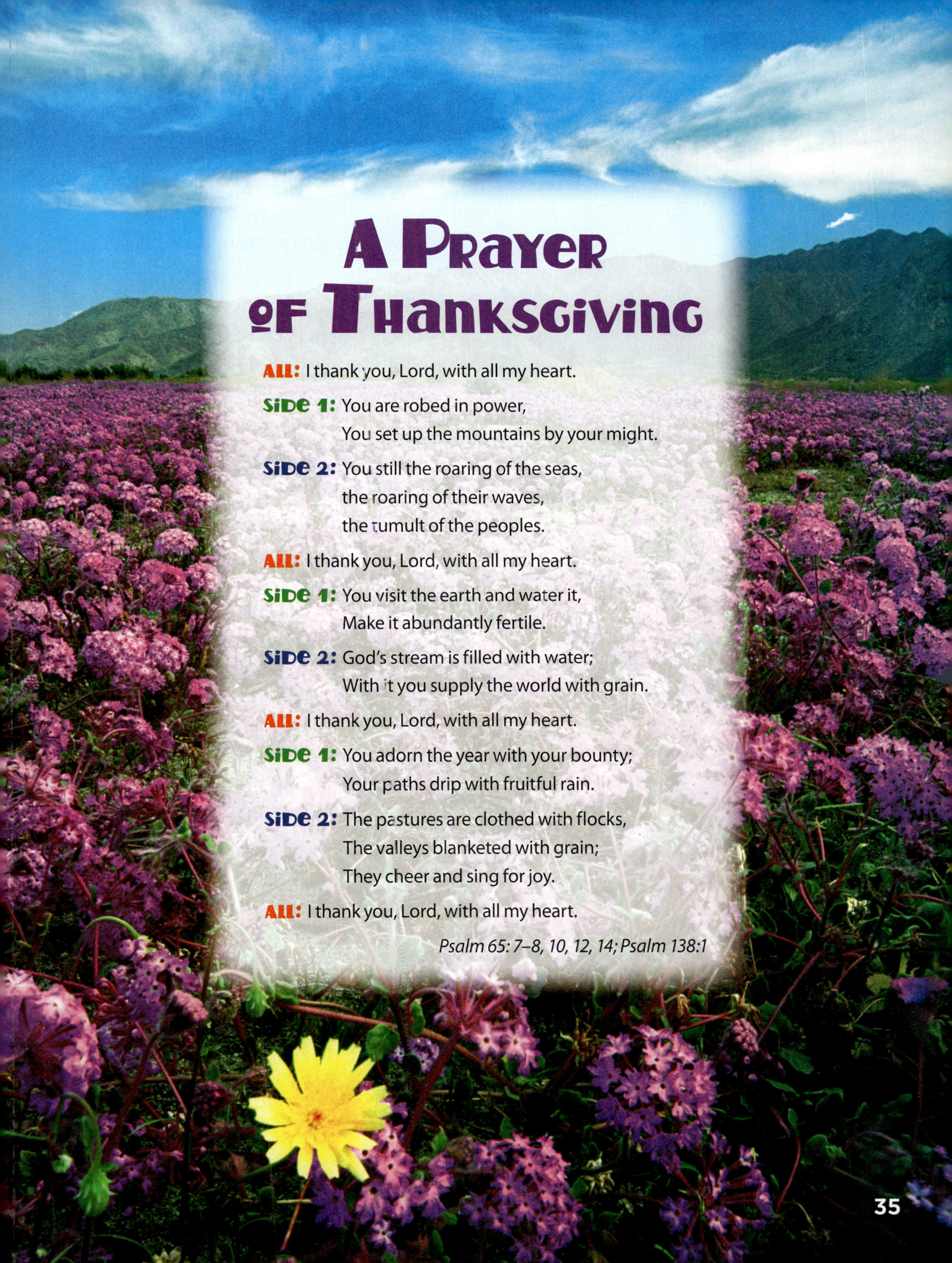

A Prayer of Thanksgiving

All: I thank you, Lord, with all my heart.

Side 1: You are robed in power,
You set up the mountains by your might.

Side 2: You still the roaring of the seas,
the roaring of their waves,
the tumult of the peoples.

All: I thank you, Lord, with all my heart.

Side 1: You visit the earth and water it,
Make it abundantly fertile.

Side 2: God's stream is filled with water;
With it you supply the world with grain.

All: I thank you, Lord, with all my heart.

Side 1: You adorn the year with your bounty;
Your paths drip with fruitful rain.

Side 2: The pastures are clothed with flocks,
The valleys blanketed with grain;
They cheer and sing for joy.

All: I thank you, Lord, with all my heart.

Psalm 65: 7–8, 10, 12, 14; Psalm 138:1

Family Note

Dear Family,

I have learned that all good gifts come from God. We thank God for these gifts at Mass. We do this especially during the Eucharistic Prayer. You can help me prepare for Holy Communion by sharing some of the reasons you give God thanks and praise at Mass.

Family Chat

Talk as a family about ways everyone can practice the virtue of gratitude.

ON YOUR OWN

Make a thank-you card for a family member or friend. Tell why he or she is God's gift to you.

WITH YOUR FAMILY

The next time you eat with your family, start the meal with everyone mentioning something he or she is grateful for. Say a prayer of thanks to God.

Remembering

Do this in memory of me.
Luke 22:19

The Photo Album

Usually Greg enjoyed spending the weekend at his grandparents' house. But this time he was stressed. He had a big social studies report due on Monday.

"What's the report about?" Grandpa asked.

"President John Kennedy," Greg replied, unhappily.

Grandpa smiled. "In that case, come with me."

Curious, Greg followed his grandfather to the basement. Grandpa rummaged around until he found an old photo album.

"Here's a scrapbook I made," said Grandpa. "I was in shock when President Kennedy was shot and killed, and I wanted to remember everything that happened."

Greg was amazed by what he saw. Many pages contained pictures of John Kennedy's life and his funeral. For the first time since getting his assignment, Greg felt excited. He knew now that he would have no trouble writing a good report.

- **What memories have older family members shared with you?**
- **What helps your family remember these past events?**
- **How does your parish remember its history?**

Remembering

People remember the past in many different ways. They may keep scrapbooks and photo albums and record family events with video cameras. Many people also remember events such as birthdays, anniversaries, and holidays with special family meals.

In the time of Jesus, people didn't have the technology you have to remember the past. But they did remember and celebrate important events with special meals. Every year Jesus and his family ate the **Passover** meal as a way to remember how God saved the Jewish people from slavery in Egypt and gave them new life.

On the night before he died, Jesus ate the Passover meal with his friends. Jesus knew he would soon die and that this meal would be his Last Supper. Like the Passover lamb that was sacrificed each year, Jesus would be the new Passover lamb.

The Last Supper

The Gospel of Luke describes the actions of Jesus at the Last Supper.

> "When the hour came, he took his place at table with the apostles. He said to them, 'I have eagerly desired to eat this Passover with you before I suffer, for, I tell you, I shall not eat it again until there is fulfillment in the kingdom of God.' Then he took a cup, gave thanks, and said, 'Take this and share it among yourselves; for I tell you from this time on I shall not drink of the fruit of the vine until the kingdom of God comes.' Then he took the bread, said the blessing, broke it, and gave it to them, saying, 'This is my body, which will be given up for you; do this in memory of me.' And likewise the cup after they had eaten, saying, 'This cup is the new covenant in my blood, which will be shed for you'."
>
> *Luke 22:14–20*

Jesus asks us to remember. At Mass, through the ministry of the priest, we remember by doing what Jesus did at the Last Supper. It is Christ himself, acting through the priest, that offers the Eucharistic Sacrifice.

Let's Talk

- **When Jesus blessed the bread, what did it become?**
- **When Jesus blessed the wine, what did it become?**
- **How did Jesus tell his friends to remember him?**
- **How do Catholics today remember Jesus?**

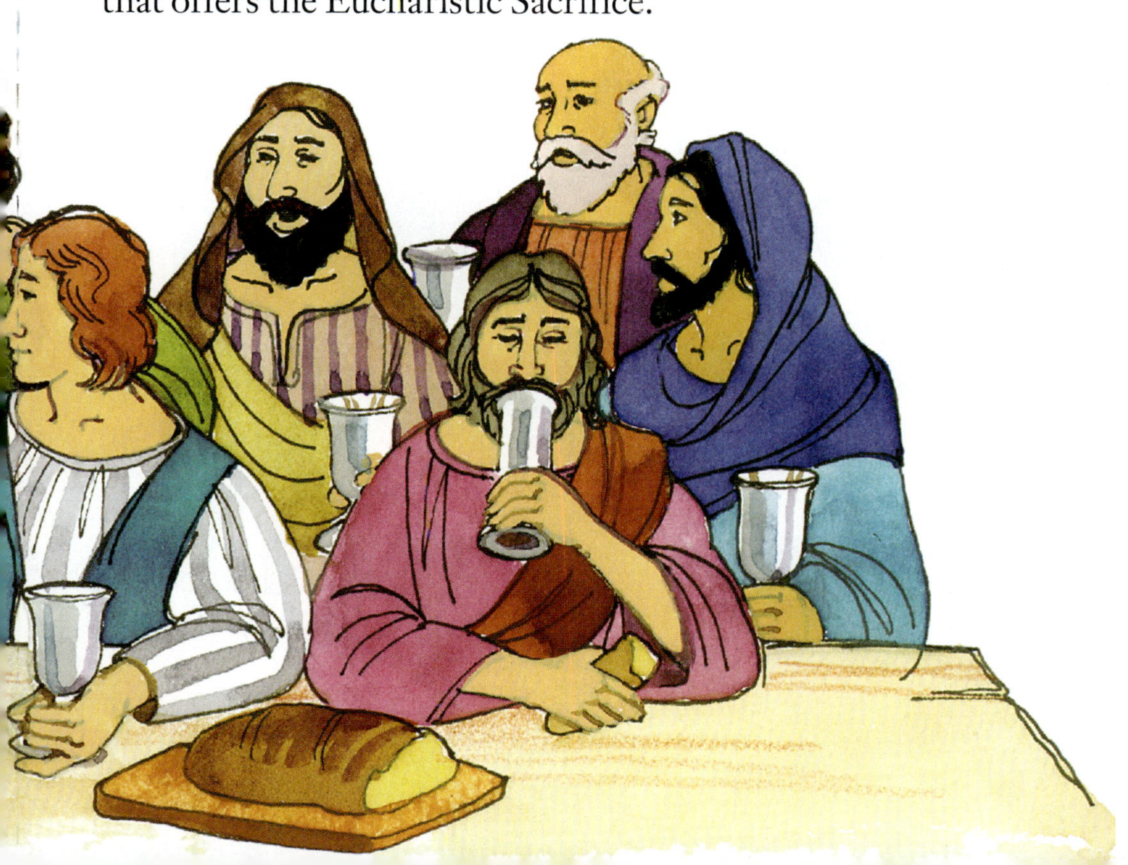

A Sacrifice of Praise

We Celebrate

Priest: Let us proclaim the mystery of faith.

People: When we eat this bread and drink this cup, we proclaim your death, Lord Jesus, until you come in glory.

At the **Last Supper,** Jesus told his disciples about the sacrifice he would make for them. A **sacrifice** is a gift to God. Jesus offered himself to God the Father by suffering and dying on the cross. Jesus offered to his Father an act of praise by doing his will.

Jesus sacrificed himself on the cross in order to free people from the slavery of sin. Three days after his death, Jesus rose to new life. He promised to give this new life to everyone who believed in him.

At Mass when we give thanks for the sacrifice of Jesus, we also bring our own lives, our prayers, and our work to God the Father.

The Eucharist is both a meal of remembering and a meal of sacrifice. The Eucharist is offered to make up for the sins of the living and the dead and to receive spiritual blessings from God. During the Eucharistic Prayer, the priest says what Jesus said at the Last Supper. The priest blesses the bread and says, "This is my Body." He then takes the cup of wine and says, "This is my Blood." Through the power of the Holy Spirit, the bread and wine truly become the Body and Blood of Christ. This part of the Eucharistic prayer is called the **consecration**. To *consecrate* means "to make something holy, to set it aside exclusively for God."

The words of consecration at Mass remind you of the loving sacrifice Jesus made. You respond by saying, "Christ has died. Christ is risen. Christ will come again." This response of faith is called the **Memorial Acclamation**.

This We Believe

The Eucharist remembers the sacrifice of Jesus and makes it present. The bread and wine truly become the Body and Blood of Christ.

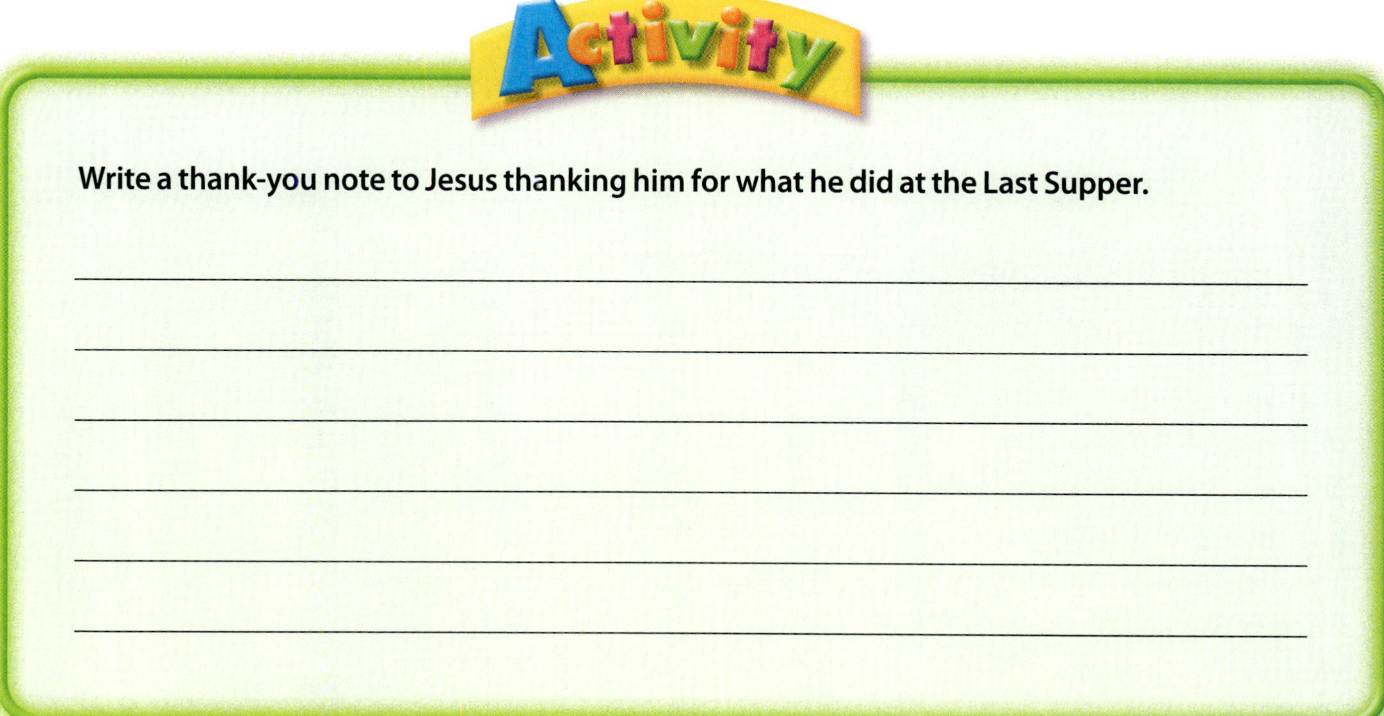

Unselfish Love

Jesus sacrificed himself out of love for us. When you love others, you are willing to be unselfish, to make sacrifices for them. Like Jesus, you give up something for the sake of a greater good.

In the cross below, write the name of a family member or friend. Then write how you can show unselfish love for this person.

For ____________________

"Whoever wishes to come after me must deny himself, take up his cross, and follow me."
Matthew 16:24

How I can show unselfish love:

____

____

____

____

____

____

____

Catholic Practices

We remember the sacrifice of Jesus at every Mass. We also remember it in a special way during the Easter Triduum on Holy Thursday, Good Friday, and the Easter Vigil on Holy Saturday.

We Remember and Give Thanks

Reader 1: Father, calling to mind the death your Son endured for our salvation, his glorious resurrection and ascension into heaven, and ready to greet him when he comes again, we offer you in thanksgiving this holy and living sacrifice.

All: Amen, alleluia, amen!

Reader 2: Look with favor on your Church's offering, and see the Victim whose death has reconciled us to yourself. Grant that we, who are nourished by his body and blood, may be filled with his Holy Spirit, and become one body, one spirit in Christ.

All: Amen, alleluia, amen!

Reader 3: Lord, may this sacrifice, which has made our peace with you, advance the peace and salvation of all the world. Through him, with him, in him, in the unity of the Holy Spirit, all glory and honor is yours, almighty Father, for ever and ever.

All: Amen, alleluia, amen!

Family Note

Dear Family,

I have learned about the sacrifice Jesus made for us. We remember and give God thanks for this sacrifice at every Mass. You can help me prepare for Holy Communion by helping me learn the different Memorial Acclamations that are said after the words of consecration.

ON YOUR OWN

Recall two things you do or say at Mass to help you remember what Jesus did.

Family Chat

Share with your child what you remember learning about Jesus.

WITH YOUR FAMILY

Decide on a sacrifice you can make together. Remember that your family is "the church of the home." This sacrifice might be giving up a meal out or not seeing the latest movie. Give the money you save to a food pantry, shelter for the poor, or some other worthwhile cause.

Go Online! www.mhbenziger.com

Sharing a Holy Meal

Learn to savor how good the Lord is.
Psalm 34:9

The Cafeteria

Jason was especially hungry as he stood in the cafeteria line. Eagerly, he reached into his pocket to see how much money he had. When his fingers found nothing, he groaned. He had forgotten to ask his dad for money this morning.

Embarrassed, Jason asked several classmates to lend him some money. "No way," they replied. "Why should we help you?"

No one would help him. Finally, Jason sat down at a table, completely humiliated and angry. His tray was empty except for a glass of water and a few packages of crackers.

"You on a diet?" asked Peter, a student he barely knew.

"Yeah, something like that," Jason replied, too proud to admit his problem.

"Too bad," Peter said as he cut his pizza in two. "I was hoping somebody would help me eat this. I had a huge breakfast, and I'd hate to see it go to waste."

Jason's stomach growled as he eyed the pizza. "Well, if you're really not going to eat it, I suppose I could," said Jason timidly.

"Great," Peter said, handing him the pizza.

Jason savored every bite. As they talked, he realized how lucky he was.

- **Why do you think Jason considered himself lucky?**
- **Talk about a time when someone shared with you. How did this kindness make you feel?**

Sharing With Others

Just like Jason and just like you, Jesus ate a lot of meals with others. Some meals were planned ahead of time while others were spur-of-the-moment, like the one in this Gospel story.

> "Jesus went up on the mountain, and there he sat down with his disciples. The Jewish feast of Passover was near. When Jesus raised his eyes and saw that a large crowd was coming to him, he said to Philip, 'Where can we buy enough food for them to eat?' He said this to test him, because he himself knew what he was going to do. Philip answered him, 'Two hundred days' wages worth of food would not be enough for each of them to have a little [bit].' One of his disciples, Andrew, the brother of Simon Peter, said to him, 'There is a boy here who has five barley loaves and two fish; but what good are these for so many?'"

"Jesus said, 'Have the people recline.' Now there was a great deal of grass in that place. So the men reclined, about five thousand in number. Then Jesus took the loaves, gave thanks, and distributed them to those who were reclining, and also as much of the fish as they wanted. When they had had their fill, he said to his disciples, 'Gather the fragments left over, so that nothing will be wasted.' So they collected them and filled twelve wicker baskets with fragments from the five barley loaves that had been more than they could eat.' "

John 6:3–13

Let's Talk

- What was the problem Jesus faced? What did he do?
- What happened when Jesus shared the boy's bread and fish with the people?
- What does this event teach us about Jesus?

A Meal of Sharing

This We Believe

When we receive Communion, we are receiving the Body and Blood of Christ. He is fully present in the Eucharist.

There is something about sharing a meal that brings people closer together. The Eucharist is a meal of sharing. At Mass when you receive **Holy Communion**, the Body and Blood of Christ, you become "one with" him and with the Church. The word *communion* means "one with."

The Communion rite begins when you and the rest of the assembly pray the **Lord's Prayer**. This prayer reminds us that God is the Father of us all. We are all brothers and sisters, members of one family.

Next you share a **Sign of Peace** with the people near you. You show that you want to be one with them. Then you say a prayer called the **Lamb of God**. You ask God for his mercy and for the peace only Jesus gives us.

We Celebrate

Lord, I am not worthy to receive you, but only say the word and I shall be healed.

When you go up to receive communion, the consecrated bread is offered with the words, "The Body of Christ." You say, "Amen." This response means you believe the Eucharist is really the Body and Blood of Christ. Then you receive the host in your hand or on your tongue.

When you receive from the cup, the consecrated wine is offered with the words, "The Blood of Christ." You say, "Amen." which means that you believe that Christ is truly present. Then you drink from the cup.

Turn to page 85 in "A Little Catechism" to review the Precepts of the Church. These important rules teach you what is expected of you as a member of the Church.

Read "How to Receive Eucharist" in *A Little Catechism* on page 83. Then work with a partner to practice receiving Holy Communion. Your partner takes the role of Eucharistic minister. **Practice walking up and receiving Eucharist.**

A Sharing Site

Pretend you are starting a club that promotes sharing with the poor. In the space below, create a home page for an Internet Web site for your club.

Parish Connection

Eucharistic ministers also take Holy Communion to the sick at home or in the hospital. This action shows we are one with all parish members.

Catholic Practices

As a sign of respect and reverence, Catholics fast before receiving Holy Communion. We do not eat or drink anything, unless it is water or medicine, for one hour before Communion.

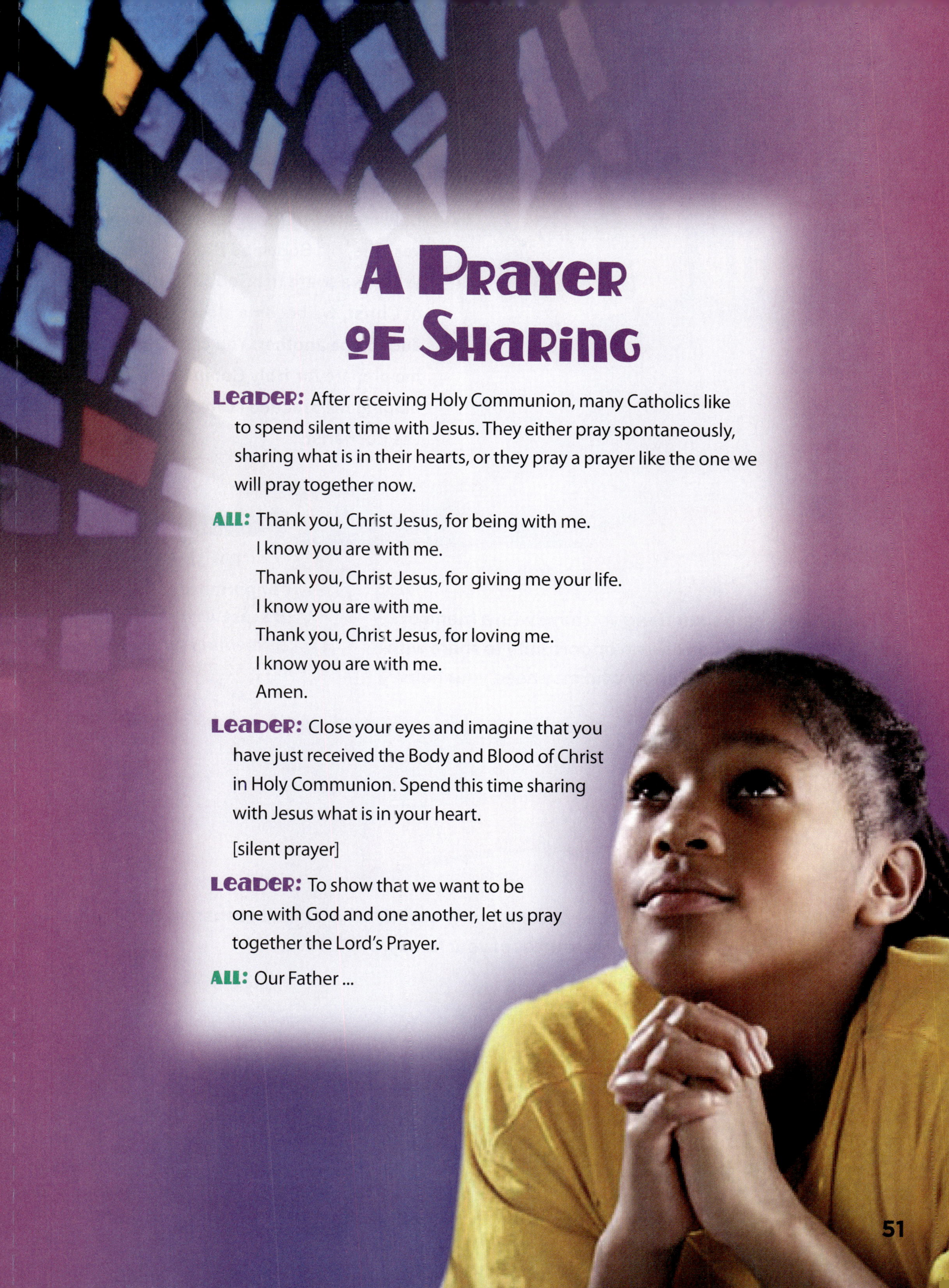

A Prayer of Sharing

Leader: After receiving Holy Communion, many Catholics like to spend silent time with Jesus. They either pray spontaneously, sharing what is in their hearts, or they pray a prayer like the one we will pray together now.

All: Thank you, Christ Jesus, for being with me.
I know you are with me.
Thank you, Christ Jesus, for giving me your life.
I know you are with me.
Thank you, Christ Jesus, for loving me.
I know you are with me.
Amen.

Leader: Close your eyes and imagine that you have just received the Body and Blood of Christ in Holy Communion. Spend this time sharing with Jesus what is in your heart.

[silent prayer]

Leader: To show that we want to be one with God and one another, let us pray together the Lord's Prayer.

All: Our Father ...

Family Note

Dear Family,

I have learned that the Eucharist is a holy meal of sharing. Jesus shares his very life, his Body and Blood with us. When we share the Body and Blood of Christ, we become closer to him and to one another. You can help me prepare for Holy Communion by helping me practice correctly receiving the Eucharist.

Family Chat

Talk about the importance of sharing. Discuss ways each family member can share.

ON YOUR OWN

This week share something you have with a friend or family member. Look for an opportunity to share with someone you do not know who may need your help.

WITH YOUR FAMILY

Take part in a parish or community activity which involves sharing the time, talent, and resources of your family.

Serving Others

Serve one another through love.
Galatians 5:13

The Parish Carnival

Amy became excited when she saw the church parking lot. It had been totally transformed with amusement rides and over fifty different booths of games and food.

Amy's class had been assigned to run the cake walk. The students were to take turns working the booth one hour at a time. When Amy's shift started, she was a bit nervous. It was her first time helping at the carnival.

The cake walk was like "musical chairs." The person left in the last space at the end won a delicious cake. Amy had plenty to do—collecting tickets, making sure each contestant had a plate, and turning the CD player on and off.

When her shift ended, Amy thought about the time she had given as a volunteer. She thought about the contribution she had made to the success of the Parish Carnival. As she walked to the volunteer tent to sign up for another hour, she thought about all the fun she had had as well.

- How did Amy's service help the parish?
- Why do you think Amy signed up to work again?
- Talk about a time when you volunteered to help out. How did you feel about helping?

Loving Service

Word of God

Whoever serves me must follow me, and where I am, there also will my servant be.

John 12:26

Jesus helped others in many ways. He cured the sick, forgave sinners, taught the ignorant, and welcomed people no one else liked. At his Last Supper, Jesus showed his disciples how he wanted all his followers to love and serve others.

"Jesus rose from supper and took off his outer garments. He took a towel and tied it around his waist. Then he poured water into a basin and began to wash the disciples' feet and dry them with the towel around his waist. He came to Simon Peter, who said to him, 'Master, are you going to wash my feet?' Jesus

answered and said to him, 'What I am doing, you do not understand now, but you will understand later.' Peter said to him, 'You will never wash my feet.' Jesus answered him, 'Unless I wash you, you will have no inheritance with me.' Simon Peter said to him, 'Master, then not only my feet, but my hands and head as well.'

"So when he had washed their feet and put his garments back on and reclined at the table again, he said to them, 'Do you realize what I have done for you? You call me "teacher" and "master," and rightly so, for indeed I am. If I, therefore, the master and teacher, have washed your feet, you ought to wash one another's feet. I have given you a model to follow, so that as I have done for you, you should also do.'"

John 13:4–9, 12–15

Let's Talk

- What did Jesus mean when he said, "you ought to wash one another's feet"?
- Based on Jesus' own example, what kind of attitude does he want you to have when you help others?
- What are ways that Christians can follow the model of Jesus today?

We Act Like Jesus

At the Last Supper, Jesus gave his disciples a **mission**, or special job. He told them to follow his example, to show God's love by serving others. The same thing happens at Mass today. The Eucharist fills you with God's love. You receive **grace**, a share in God's own life, so that, inspired by the Holy Spirit, you can serve others every day. This is following the model of Jesus. As disciples of Jesus in the Church, we are a sign of God's love for all.

The word *Mass* means "sent." As Mass ends, the priest sends you out to act like Jesus in today's world. You receive a mission to serve others in love.

Most of the time, serving others consists of helping in ordinary ways at home and at school. You are called to acts of love for members of your family. You are called to acts of kindness and caring for the people you are with during the day. This is following the model of Jesus.

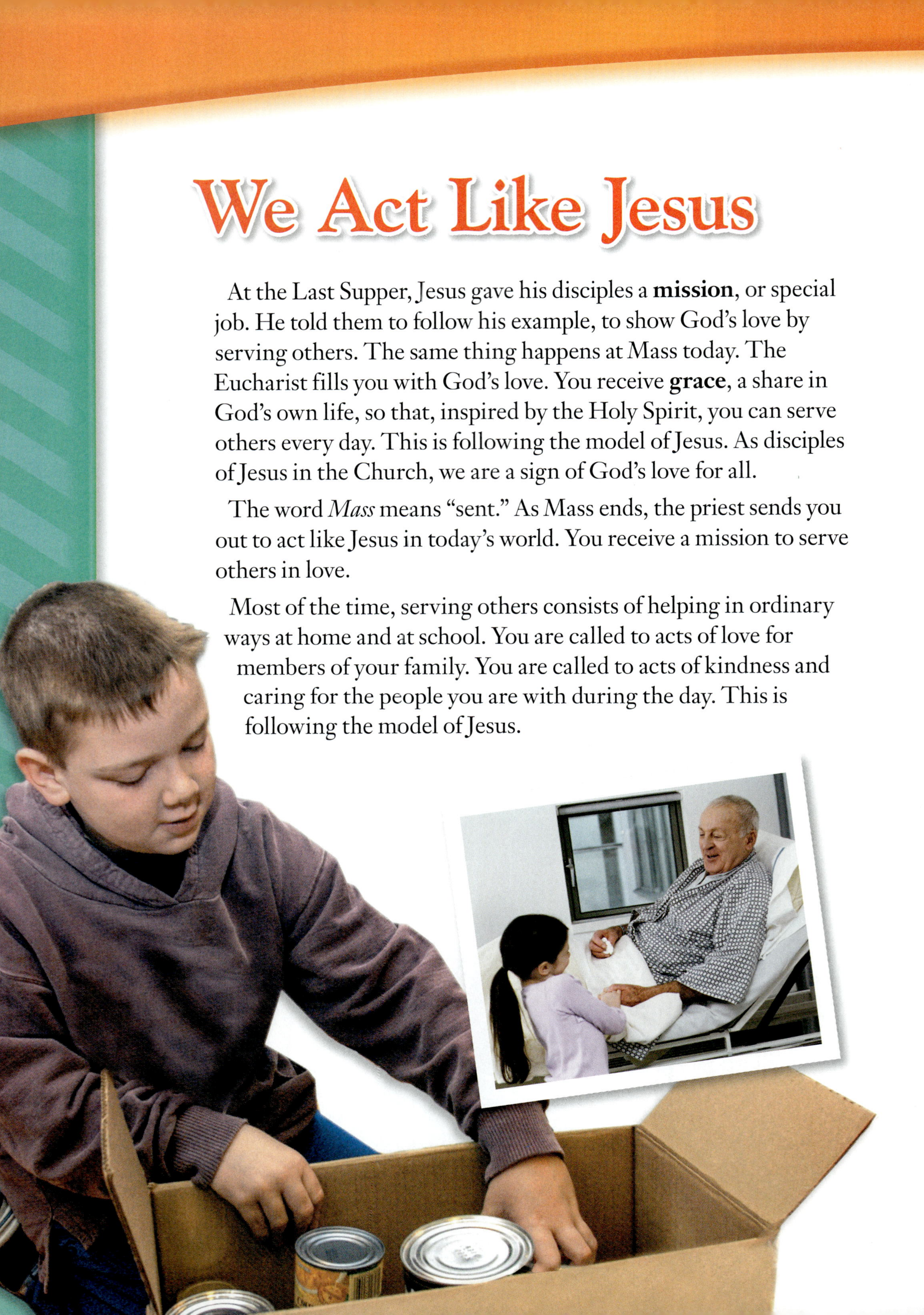

Your Mission

The mission you receive at Mass occurs after Communion, when the priest gives the final **blessing**. He says, "May almighty God bless you, the Father, and the Son, and the Holy Spirit." You and everyone assembled make the Sign of the Cross and say, "Amen."

Then the priest says, "Go in peace to love and serve the Lord." You answer, "Thanks be to God."

The Mass is over, but the effects of the Eucharist continue through your words, actions, and attitudes. Jesus is with you every day during the week. He helps you love and serve everyone you meet.

This We Believe

The Mass sends us out to love and serve others.

Activity

Look at the pictures on these two pages. **Tell how each person is acting "to love and serve the Lord."**

Serving Others

Think of someone you can serve at home, school, or in your parish. This might be a parent, teacher, or someone in need. Create a service coupon book. Each coupon is good for one act of kindness which you promise to give. Here are some examples.

Catholic Practices

Catholic parishes collect money, food, and clothing to help the poor. When you give in these ways, you love and serve the Lord.

The holder of this coupon may redeem it for:

____

I promise to do this act of service.

Signed: ______________________________

The holder of this coupon may redeem it for:

____

Signed: ______________________________

The holder of this coupon may redeem it for:

____

Signed: ______________________________

We Love and Serve

Leader: Heavenly Father, you know there are many needs in today's world. Fill us with your love so that we may serve as Jesus did. Hear us as we pray together this prayer of your faithful servant, Saint Francis.

All: Lord, make me an instrument of your peace.
where there is hatred, let me sow love;
where there is injury, pardon;
where there is doubt, faith;
where there is despair, hope;
where there is darkness, light;
where there is sadness, joy.

Oh divine Master, grant that I may not so much seek
to be consoled as to console,
to be understood as to understand,
to be loved as to love.
For it is in giving that we receive,
it is in pardoning that we are pardoned,
it is in dying that we are born to eternal life.

Saint Francis of Assisi

Family Note

Dear Family,

I have learned that Jesus served his disciples by washing their feet. Jesus wants us to follow his example by serving others. You can help me prepare for Holy Communion by discussing how the Eucharist strengthens you to love and serve others each day.

Family Chat

Discuss the attitudes Christians should have when they serve others.

ON YOUR OWN

Make a calendar for this week. On each day write one way you will serve others at home, at school, or in the community. Then carry out your plan.

WITH YOUR FAMILY

Decide on one way family members can work together to meet a need in your parish, town, or neighborhood.

 Go Online! www.mhbenziger.com

Living Eucharist

This is my body, which will be given for you; do this in memory of me.

Luke 22:19

A Day to Remember

Your First Communion is a holy day that you will always remember! You received the Body and Blood of Christ for the first time! You are in a "holy communion" with Jesus and with his community, the Church.

Remembering this holy day and all you did to prepare for the celebration will help you better understand the Eucharist.

- My favorite part of preparing for First Communion was ...
- I learned about the many meals Jesus had with friends and strangers. One story I remember is ...
- As my First Communion drew near, I remember feeling ...

We Remember

The whole Church in heaven and on earth rejoices that you have received Christ in the Eucharist. Remember what it was like when you arrived at church on that special day. Remember the people, the sights, the sounds, the songs, the story, the meal.

As you recall each part of the Mass, tell why each is important. This will give you a deeper understanding of the sacrament you celebrated.

Gathering

The Eucharist begins when God's people gather together to worship God.

What do you remember about first arriving at Church? Who was with you? How did you feel?

Liturgy of the Word

God speaks to us in the Liturgy of the Word.

Picture yourself sitting and listening to God's Word being proclaimed. What words or thoughts do you remember?

Liturgy of the Eucharist

During the Eucharistic Prayer, you and the whole Church knelt in prayer as we remembered the story of Jesus' Last Supper.

He broke the bread, gave it to his disciples and said, "This is my Body." He took the cup and said, "This is my Blood."

The bread and wine became the Body and Blood of Christ.

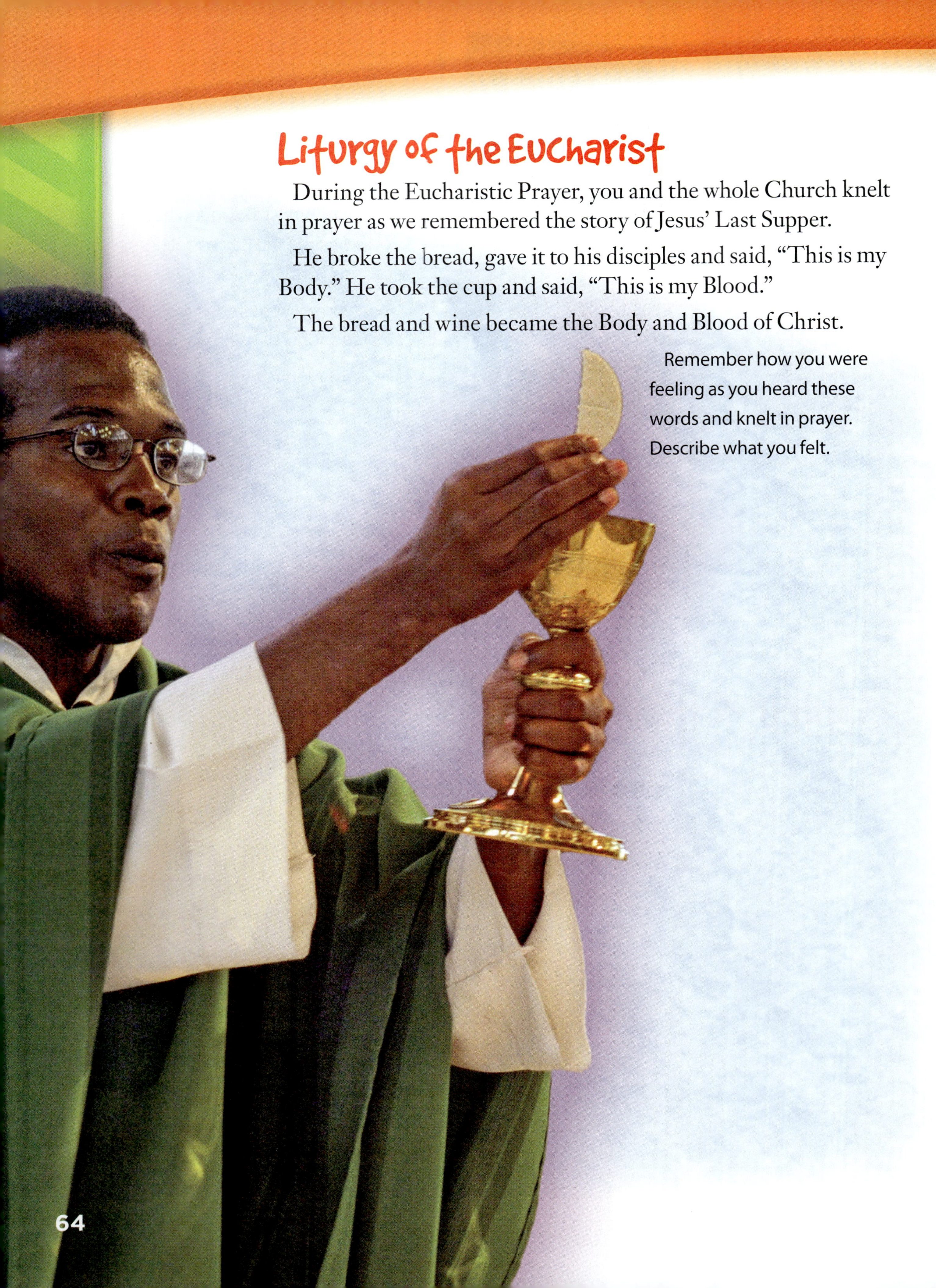

Remember how you were feeling as you heard these words and knelt in prayer. Describe what you felt.

Communion Rite

We are united with Christ and with one another in Holy Communion.

Imagine yourself as you received the Body and Blood of Christ for the first time. What did you feel? What was in your heart?

Dismissal

We are sent forth to continue doing the good work of Jesus.

What were you feeling as you left the church?

What did you and your family do after you left church?

Your Mission

The Eucharist gives you strength to go out and do the work of Jesus. The priest sends you forth in mission to tell others the Good News. He says at the end of Mass, "Go forth to love and serve the Lord."

How will you go forth to love and serve the Lord?

How has your First Communion made you a better follower of Jesus?

A Great Banquet

When you give a banquet, invite the poor, the crippled, the lame and the blind.

Luke 14:13

Leader: The Eucharist is a special meal, a great banquet, a sacred feast for the Church. You have come to the table of the Lord. You are one of Jesus' chosen disciples and you now have a place at the table.

Sit silently and imagine the great banquet as I read the story from the Bible.

Read the story of the Great Banquet. (Luke 14:7-14)

Reflection: How does celebrating First Communion help you to serve the poor, the crippled, the lame and the blind? Give an example.

Leader: Together let us pray:

Dear Jesus,

Thank you for giving me yourself in holy communion. Eucharist has brought me closer to you. May the Eucharist strengthen me to be a better disciple. Amen.

Family Note

Dear Family,

I have learned that Eucharist is a holy mystery. My First Communion helped me to better understand this mystery. My First Communion united me with Jesus and my community.

Family Chat

What does Eucharist mean to you?

Think about the different parts of your First Communion celebration. Close your eyes and imagine you are back in that day again. What does it mean?

WITH YOUR FAMILY

Get out the pictures from First Communion. Talk about why it was an important day and what makes it so holy? How does Eucharist make your family better disciples?

Go Online! www.mhbenziger.com

Then he took the bread, said the blessing, broke it, and gave it to them, saying, "This is my body, which will be given for you; do this in memory of me."

from Luke 22: 19

- *We Believe*
- *We Celebrate*
- *We Live*
- *We Pray*

We Believe

It is important to have the right words to talk about your faith. When you use the right words, you can share your faith with others. Here is a list of some of the things you have learned. As you grow older, you will learn more and more about these beliefs.

1. The Blessed Trinity is three Persons in one God: God the Father, God the Son, and God the Holy Spirit. There is only one God, but God is three Persons. You can say, "I believe in God—Father, Son, and Holy Spirit."

2. Jesus is the Son of God, the only Son of the Father. God loved his people so much that he sent his Son, Jesus, to die for our sins. Jesus became man and came to Earth to show us the Father's love and to save all people.

3. The name Jesus means "God saves." Jesus saved us by his passion, death, Resurrection, and Ascension. This is called the Paschal Mystery.

4. The Paschal Mystery, Jesus' passion, death, Resurrection, and Ascension, is made present in the celebration of the Eucharist. Its saving effects are carried on through the sacraments of the Church.

5. Jesus will come again at the end of time to judge those living and those who have died.

6. God made us to love him and it is only with God that we will find true happiness.

7. The gift of the Holy Spirit was given to the Church. The Holy Spirit works with the Father and the Son to guide the Church.

8. The Apostles taught the people all that Jesus had taught them. The Church carries on the work of Jesus today with the help of the Holy Spirit.

9. The Church is the People of God, the Body of Christ. Those nourished by the Body of Christ become the Body of Christ. The Church shares the Good News of Jesus Christ with others. Those nourished with the Body of Christ become the Body of Christ.

10. The Church teaches the Law of God. Catholics follow the teachings of the Church, especially the teachings of the pope, and the bishops together with the pope.

11. The Holy Spirit guides the Church and helps keep the followers of Jesus faithful to the truth. The Church is the temple of the Holy Spirit.

12. Those who follow Jesus know that they are called to serve one another in love and to share the message of Jesus with others.

13. Jesus gives many gifts and the best gift is a share in God's own life, which is called grace.

14. The Risen Jesus is with the People of God in the Eucharist and in the other sacraments.

15. God created us. Our lives are good. Every gift we have comes from God. We are free and can make choices.

16. By Baptism we become adopted children of God through Jesus Christ.

17. God has given every person the gift of free will. This freedom makes people responsible for the choices they make.

18. We respond to God's love by keeping his commandments and by trying with all our hearts to be faithful, to respect all life, and to do what is right.

19. Mary is the Mother of God and our mother, too. We turn to Mary in prayer—she will help us.

20. Prayer is lifting one's mind and heart to God. In prayer we praise God, ask God to help us, and give thanks to God for his gifts. We also pray for other people. Prayer is the best way to stay on the right path.

Important Questions

The questions and answers below will help you remember what you learn as you prepare for the Sacraments of Reconciliation and Eucharist. Try to learn the answers by heart.

1. *Why are the Gospels so important?*

The four Gospels are important because they tell about Jesus Christ—his life and his teachings.

2. *What is a conscience?*

A conscience is the ability to know what is right and to do what is right. God's Law and the teaching of the Church helps to form a correct conscience.

3. *How does sin affect a person's relationship with God?*

Sin is an offense against God and his Law. Sin is choosing to turn away from God. Mortal sin breaks a person's relationship with God.

4. *Which sacrament helps people heal their relationship with God?*

The Sacrament of Reconciliation, or Penance, celebrates God's loving forgiveness.

5. *Why is the Eucharist the heart of Catholic life?*

The night before he died, Jesus gave us the Eucharist by sharing himself, Body and Blood, with his friends under the appearance of bread and wine. Jesus continues to be present today in the Mass—in the people gathered, in the Word of God, in the person of the priest, and especially in the consecrated bread and wine which have become the Body and Blood of Christ.

6. *What mission do you receive at the end of Mass?*

I am sent to love and to serve the Lord.

Things to Remember

The Gifts of the Holy Spirit

- Wisdom
- Understanding
- Knowledge
- Counsel
- Piety
- Fortitude
- Fear of the Lord

Spiritual Works of Mercy

- Help the sinner.
- Teach the ignorant.
- Counsel the doubtful.
- Bear wrongs patiently.
- Forgive injuries.
- Pray for the living and the dead.

Corporal Works of Mercy

- Feed the hungry.
- Give drink to the thirsty.
- Clothe the naked.
- Shelter the homeless.
- Visit the sick.
- Visit the imprisoned.
- Bury the dead.

The Great Commandment

You shall love the Lord, your God, with all your heart, with all your soul, and with all your mind. You shall love your neighbor as yourself.

We Celebrate

Sacraments

The seven sacraments are outward signs and celebrations of God's love and life, or grace. The sacraments communicate and share God's life as the gift of grace. Through the sacraments you give worship and praise to God, grow in holiness, work to build up God's reign on Earth, and strengthen the unity of God's People.

Christian initiation happens in three sacraments together: Baptism, which is the beginning of new life in Christ; Confirmation, which is its strengthening; and Eucharist, which nourishes you with Christ's Body and Blood to become more like Jesus. Reconciliation and Anointing of the Sick are Sacraments of Healing. Holy Orders and Matrimony are Sacraments at the Service of Communion.

Baptism

You are freed from original sin and from all sin. You are given the new life of grace, by which you become an adopted child of God, one with Christ in the Holy Spirit, and a member of the Church. Baptism imprints a spiritual mark on your soul that claims you for Christ. Baptism can only be received once.

Confirmation

The gift of the Holy Spirit strengthens you to live as Jesus did. As in Baptism, your soul is imprinted with a spiritual mark as a sign of the Holy Spirit's presence. The Holy Spirit will help you by word and action to witness to Christ.

Eucharist

In Eucharist Christ is truly present in the consecrated bread and wine. To receive communion you must be in the state of grace. You are encouraged to receive communion every time you go to Mass.

Reconciliation or Penance

When you are sorry for your sins, God offers you pardon and peace through the words and actions of a priest.

Anointing of the Sick

A priest anoints a person who is sick or elderly and offers God's healing comfort and forgiveness.

Holy Orders

The Church ordains deacons, priests, and bishops to teach, to lead, to celebrate, to guide, and to serve the People of God.

Matrimony

A man and a woman promise to live their whole lives as husband and wife and become a sign of God's love.

The Celebration of the Eucharist

When the hour came, Jesus took his place at table with the Apostles. He said to them, "I have eagerly wanted to eat this Passover with you before I suffer. I won't eat it again until there is fulfillment in the kingdom of God."

Then Jesus took the bread, said the blessing, broke it, and gave it to them, saying, "This is my body, which will be given for you. Do this in memory of me." In the same way, he took the cup after they had eaten. He said, "This cup is the new covenant in my blood, which will be shed for you."

From Luke 22:14-20

At Mass, followers of Jesus all around the world come to worship and praise God, and to remember the actions of Jesus at the Last Supper. They listen to and learn from the reading of God's Living Word.

They remember and relive the great love of Jesus who gave up his life for all people. They share in that love by receiving the Body and Blood of Christ in Holy Communion. Finally, they go to their homes in peace, knowing that they are called to love and to serve others.

Introductory Rites

At the beginning of Mass, the People of God are gathered with Christ and with one another. We prepare to worship God.

Entrance Procession We stand as the priest and other ministers process into the assembly. We join in singing an entrance song.

Greeting

Priest: In the name of the Father, and of the Son, and of the Holy Spirit.

People: Amen.

Priest: The grace and peace of God our Father and the Lord Jesus Christ be with you.

People: And also with you.

Penitential Rite We praise God for his mercy.

Priest: Lord, have mercy.

People: Lord, have mercy.

Priest: Christ, have mercy.

People: Christ, have mercy.

Priest: Lord, have mercy.

People: Lord, have mercy.

Gloria On most Sundays we pray the Gloria, a hymn of praise.

Glory to God in the highest,
and peace to his people on earth.

Lord God, heavenly King,
almighty God and Father,
we worship you, we give you thanks,
we praise you for your glory.

Lord Jesus Christ, only Son of the Father,

Lord God, Lamb of God,
you take away the sin of the world:
have mercy on us;

you are seated at the right hand of the father:
receive our prayer.

For you alone are the Holy One,

you alone are the Lord,

you alone are the Most High,
Jesus Christ,
with the Holy Spirit,
in the glory of God the Father.
Amen.

Opening Prayer We observe a moment of silence and lift up our hearts and minds to God. The priest leads us in prayer.

Priest: Let us pray…

People: Amen.

Liturgy of the Word

We listen to the Word of God.

First Reading This reading is taken from the Old Testament or, during the Easter season, from the Acts of the Apostles. At the end of the reading the reader says:

Reader: The Word of the Lord.

People: Thanks be to God.

Responsorial Psalm The cantor leads us in singing a psalm.

Second Reading The second reading is taken from the letters in the New Testament or from the Acts of the Apostles. At the end of the reading the reader says:

Reader: The Word of the Lord.

People: Thanks be to God.

Alleluia or Gospel Acclamation

As we sing the Alleluia we show reverence for Jesus, the Word of God. We stand to show that we believe Jesus is with us in the Gospel. During Lent we do not sing the Alleluia. We sing a different Scripture verse from the Gospel reading.

Gospel

Priest or deacon: The Lord be with you.

People: And also with you.

Priest or deacon: A reading from the Gospel according to (name of the Gospel writer).

People: Glory to you, Lord.

Priest or deacon (at the end of the Gospel): The Gospel of the Lord.

People: Praise to you, Lord Jesus Christ.

Homily The priest or deacon helps the community to understand and live the Scripture that has been proclaimed.

Profession of Faith We stand and profess our faith. We pray the Nicene Creed. (See page 89) When we pray the creed we are saying what we believe.

General Intercessions We pray for the needs of the Church, for public leaders, for the salvation of the world, and for the needs of people. After each petition we might respond:

People: Lord, hear our prayer.

Liturgy of the Eucharist

We give thanks and praise.

Preparation of the Altar and Gifts We sit as the gifts of bread and wine are brought up and the altar is prepared.

The priest lifts up the bread and says:

Priest: Blessed are you, Lord,
God of all creation,
Through your goodness we have this bread to offer, which earth has given and human hands have made.
It will become for us the bread of life.

People: Blessed be God forever.

The priest lifts up the chalice of wine and prays:

Priest: Blessed are you, Lord,
God of all creation.
through your goodness we have
this wine to offer,
fruit of the vine and work of human hands.
It will become our spiritual drink.

People: Blessed be God for ever.

Priest: Pray, my brothers and sisters, that our sacrifice may be acceptable to God, the almighty Father.

We stand to say the following prayer.

People: May the Lord accept the sacrifice at your hands for the praise and glory of his name, for our good, and the good of all his Church.

Prayer over the Gifts The priest says a prayer over the gifts.

People: Amen.

Eucharistic Prayer The priest invites us to give thanks and praise.

Priest: The Lord be with you.

People: And also with you.

Priest: Lift up your hearts.

People: We lift them up to the Lord.

Priest: Let us give thanks to the Lord our God.

People: It is right to give him thanks and praise.

After the priest says the preface, a prayer that gives a special reason for praising God, we join in saying or singing the acclamation.

All: Holy, holy, holy Lord,
God of power and might,
heaven and Earth are full of your glory.
Hosanna in the highest.
Blessed is he who comes
in the name of the Lord.
Hosanna in the highest.

The "Holy, holy, holy" is followed by a prayer asking that the power of Holy Spirit might come upon the gifts and make them holy, that is, become the Body and Blood of Christ, and that those who receive these gifts might be transformed into Christ.

At the consecration the bread and wine become the Body and Blood of the Lord through the power of the Holy Spirit and the words of the priest. Jesus is truly present in the bread and wine that we receive at Communion.

After the consecration, we pray or sing the memorial acclamation.

Priest or deacon: Let us proclaim the mystery of faith.

People: Christ has died, Christ is risen, Christ will come again.

The priest prays for the Church and for the living and the dead and that one day we will live in heaven. The doxology concludes the Eucharistic prayer.

Priest: Through him, with him, in him, in the unity of the Holy Spirit, all glory and honor is yours, almighty Father, for ever and ever.

People: Amen.

The Eucharistic prayer ends with a great "Amen," a "so be it" or a "yes" to all of the Eucharistic prayers that we make our own.

Communion Rite

The Lord's Prayer As we prepare ourselves to receive the Body and Blood of the Lord, we are invited to say the Lord's Prayer. (See page 88)

Sign of Peace We pray for peace and unity for the Church and the whole world.

Priest or deacon: The peace of the Lord be with you always.

People: And also with you.

Priest or deacon: Let us offer each other the sign of peace.

Breaking of the Bread At the Last Supper, Jesus broke the bread and gave it to his disciples. The priest breaks the consecrated host so it can be shared. While he is breaking the bread, we say or sing:

Lamb of God, you take away the sins
of the world:
have mercy on us.

Lamb of God, you take away the sins
of the world:
have mercy on us.

Lamb of God, you take away the sins
of the world:
grant us peace.

Communion The priest raises the consecrated bread and proclaims:

Priest: This is the Lamb of God who takes away the sins of the world. Happy are we who are called to his supper.

People: Lord, I am not worthy to receive you, but only say the word and I shall be healed.

The priest receives Holy Communion. We process up the aisle to receive the Body and Blood of Christ.

Priest: The Body of Christ.

People: Amen.

We receive the consecrated host in our hand or on our tongue.

Priest: The Blood of Christ.

People: Amen.

We take a sip from the cup

Prayer after Communion We stand as the priest leads us in prayer.

Priest: Let us pray.

People: Amen.

Concluding Rite

Priest: The Lord be with you.

People: And also with you.

Blessing

Priest: May almighty God bless you, the Father, and the Son, and the Holy Spirit.

People: Amen.

Dismissal At the conclusion of Mass we are sent out to help others as Jesus did.

Priest or deacon: The Mass is ended. Go in peace to love and serve the Lord.

People: Thanks be to God.

The priest kisses the altar as a sign of reverence because the table is holy and sacred to the action of the assembly gathered. He and the other ministers process out of the church while we sing a concluding hymn.

Eucharist

- Eucharist is at the heart of the life of the Church.
- The consecrated bread and wine are truly the Body and Blood of Christ.
- Jesus gave us the Eucharist at his Last Supper.
- In order to receive Holy Communion worthily, you must be free from mortal sin.
- Catholics are encouraged to receive Eucharist every time they go to Mass. Catholics are required to receive Eucharist at least once a year during the Easter season.
- Catholics fast from food and drink (except water or medicine) for one hour before receiving Communion.

How to Receive Eucharist

There are different ways to receive Holy Communion—in your hand, on your tongue, and from the cup.

If you choose to receive Holy Communion in your hand:

- Bow, hold out both hands, palms up, with one hand resting on top of the other.
- The priest or Eucharistic minister says, "The Body of Christ," and places the consecrated Host in your hand. You answer, "Amen."
- Step to one side, using the hand that is underneath, take the Host in your fingers, and place it in your mouth. Swallow the consecrated Host.

If you choose to receive Holy Communion on your tongue:

- Fold your hands in prayer. Bow.
- The priest or Eucharistic minister says, "The Body of Christ." You answer "Amen."
- Open your mouth and put your tongue out to receive the Host. Swallow the consecrated Host.

You may also receive the Blood of Christ from the cup.

- After you have received the Body of Christ, go to the priest or Eucharistic minister who is offering the cup.
- The priest or Eucharistic minister will say, "The Blood of Christ." You answer, "Amen."
- Take the cup of consecrated wine in both hands, and take a small sip. Return the cup to the minister.

After receiving Communion, return to your place and kneel or sit quietly for a few minutes, giving thanks to God.

Reconciliation

There are two ways we can celebrate the Sacrament of Reconciliation—individual or communal.

The following are the steps for individual confession.

1. **Greeting**
   - The priest greets us and we make the Sign of the Cross.
   - The priest may say these or similar words:

     May God, who has enlightened every heart, help you to know your sins and trust in his mercy. Amen.

2. **Reading of the Word of God.**
   The priest may read a passage from the Bible.

3. **Confession of Sins and Acceptance of Penance**
   - We tell our sins to the priest. We must confess mortal sins. We may also confess venial sins.
   - After we confess our sins, the priest may talk to us and advise us. Then he gives us our penance. A penance is something we do to show we are sorry and that we want to make up for our sins.

4. **Prayer of Contrition and Absolution**
   - The priest asks us to pray the Act of Contrition to tell we are sorry for our sins.
   - The priest gives absolution by extending his hands over our head and saying:

     God, the Father of mercies,
     through the death and Resurrection
     of his Son
     has reconciled the world to himself
     and sent the Holy Spirit among us
     for the forgiveness of sins;
     through the ministry of the Church
     may God give you pardon and
     peace.

   The priest makes the Sign of the Cross over our head as he says:

     and I absolve you from your sins
     in the name of the Father,
     and of the Son,
     and of the Holy Spirit.

   We make the Sign of the Cross and say, "Amen."

5. **Proclamation of Praise of God and Dismissal**
   After the absolution, the priest continues: Give thanks to the Lord, for he is good.

   We respond: His mercy endures for ever.

   The priest sends us forth saying: The Lord has freed you from your sins. Go in peace.

We Live

God's Law

Sometimes it can be hard to choose the right thing to do. Rules can help you to stay on the right track. Good rules can help you take care of yourself—inside and out. Rules help everyone make choices that lead to a happier and healthier life.

The Ten Commandments

These are ten rules for being faithful to God. Following the commandments provides a clear path for you. The Ten Commandments help you live out your covenant relationship with God.

1. I am the Lord, your God. You shall not have other gods besides me.
2. You shall not take the name of the Lord, your God, in vain.
3. Remember to keep holy the Sabbath day (the Day of the Lord).
4. Honor your father and your mother.
5. You shall not kill.
6. You shall not commit adultery.
7. You shall not steal.
8. You shall not bear false witness against your neighbor.
9. You shall not covet your neighbor's wife.
10. You shall not covet anything that belongs to your neighbor.

Good Advice

Follow the advice below to avoid temptations and make good choices.

Figure out your choices.
Rest your brain awhile, and pray.
Ease off—don't decide in a hurry.
Stop and think about the consequences.
Hold off until you are pretty sure.

Set your conscience in action.
Take it slow and easy.
Ask what Jesus would do.
Review all the facts and advice.
Then make a right choice.

The Precepts of the Church

The Church has rules that help us live the Gospel. They tell Catholics how to show love for God and for others.

1. You shall attend Mass on Sundays and on holy days of obligation. Do no unnecessary work on Sunday.
2. Receive the Sacrament of Penance (Reconciliation) once a year.
3. Receive the Eucharist (Holy Communion) at least during the Easter season.
4. Do penance (fasting and abstinence) on the appointed days.
5. Contribute to the support of the Church.

The Beatitudes

Jesus used the Beatitudes to teach people what is truly important in God's Kingdom. The Beatitudes show people how they should live and what they should treasure to be happy with God now and forever.

Blessed are the poor in spirit,
for theirs is the kingdom of heaven.
Blessed are they who mourn,
for they will be comforted.
Blessed are the meek,
for they will inherit the land.
Blessed are they who hunger and thirst for righteousness,
for they will be satisfied.
Blessed are the merciful,
for they shall be shown mercy.
Blessed are the clean of heart,
for they shall see God.
Blessed are the peacemakers,
for they will be called children of God.
Blessed are they who are persecuted for the sake of righteous,
for theirs is the kingdom of heaven.

Matthew 5:3–10

Things to Know

1. What is sin?

Sin is making a choice to do something wrong. In sin we turn our hearts away from God's love. It not only hurts our relationship with God but with one another.

There are two kinds of sin: venial and mortal.

- A venial sin is a lesser sin. It is when a person is not being as good a friend to God and to people as God wants.
- A mortal sin is a serious sin. The person completely breaks off his or her friendship with God. Mortal sin must be confessed in the Sacrament of Reconciliation.

2. What is necessary for something to be a mortal sin?

Something is a mortal sin if the act is seriously wrong, the person knows it is seriously wrong, and the person chooses to do it anyway.

3. Ask for forgiveness.

- When you have done something wrong, ask God to forgive you.
- If you have committed a serious sin, celebrate the Sacrament of Reconciliation.

An Examination of Conscience

You examine your conscience to help you live as a child of God. You ask yourself if you are living as Jesus wants you to live. You ask for the help of the Holy Spirit to be more like Jesus. Ask yourself how you act toward:

God

Do I talk to God every day?
Do I say God's name only in a prayerful way?
Have I missed Mass on Sunday through my own fault?
Am I trying to trust God like Jesus did?

Myself

Do I do things that will help me grow as God wants?
Do I take care of what I have?
Do I care for the things of the Earth?
Do I thank God for the gifts and talents God has given me?

My Family, My Friends, and Other People

Do I do my chores well, or do I have to be asked?
Do I try to do my best at school?
Do I obey my parents and show them respect?
When someone who is taking care of me asks me to do something good, do I obey?
Am I generous? Do I share what I have with others, especially those in need?
When I am angry, do I talk about it, or do I say or do things to hurt whoever hurt me?
Do I say, "I'm sorry" to the person I have hurt and "I forgive you" to the person who has hurt me?
Do I play fair, or do I ever cheat at school, work, or games?
Have I taken something that doesn't belong to me?
Do I tell the whole truth? Or do I let people believe something that isn't true?
Am I jealous of what other people have?

We Pray

Sign of the Cross

In the name of the Father,
and of the Son, and of the
Holy Spirit.
Amen.

Act of Contrition

O my God, I am sorry for my sins with all my heart. In choosing to do wrong and failing to do good, I have sinned against you whom I should love above all things. I firmly intend, with the help of your grace, to do penance, to sin no more, and to avoid whatever leads me to sin. Our Savior Jesus Christ suffered and died for us. In his name, dear God, forgive me. Amen.

Hail Mary

Hail Mary, full of grace,
the Lord is with you.
Blessed are you among women,
and blessed is the fruit
of your womb, Jesus.
Holy Mary, Mother of God,
pray for us sinners,
now and at the hour of our
death.
Amen.

Lord's Prayer

Our Father, who art in heaven,
hallowed by thy name;
thy kingdom come;
thy will be done on Earth
as it is in heaven.
Give us this day our daily bread;
and forgive us our trespasses
as we forgive those who trespass
against us;
and lead us not into temptation,
but deliver us from evil.
Amen.

Glory Be to the Father

Glory be to the Father,
and to the Son,
and to the Holy Spirit,
as it was in the beginning,
is now and ever shall be,
world without end. Amen.

The Nicene Creed

We believe in one God,
the Father, the Almighty,
maker of heaven and earth,
of all that is seen and unseen.

We believe in one Lord, Jesus Christ,
the only Son of God.
eternally begotten of the Father,
God from God, Light from Light,
true God from true God.
begotten, not made, one in Being
with the Father.
Through him all things were made.
For us men and for our salvation
he came down from heaven:

by the power of the Holy Spirit
he was born of the Virgin Mary,
and became man.

For our sake he was crucified under
Pontius Pilate;
he suffered, died, and was buried.
On the third day he rose again
in fulfillment of the Scriptures;
he ascended into heaven
and is seated at the right hand
of the Father.

He will come again in glory to judge
the living and the dead,
and his kingdom will have no end.

We believe in the Holy Spirit, the Lord,
the giver of life,
who proceeds from the Father and
the Son.
With the Father and the Son he is
worshiped and glorified.
H has spoken through the Prophets.
We believe in one holy catholic and
apostolic Church.
We acknowledge one baptism for
the forgiveness of sins.
We look for the resurrection of
the dead,
and the life of the world to come.
Amen.

I Confess (Confiteor)

I confess to almighty God,
And to you, my brothers and sisters,
That I have sinned through my own fault
In my thoughts and in my words,
In what I have done,
And in what I have failed to do;
And I ask blessed Mary, ever virgin,
All the angels and saints,
And you, my brothers and sisters,
To pray for me to the Lord our God.

Glossary

blessing A divine action that gives life. The whole of God's work is a blessing.

Catholic This word means "universal." Catholics follow the Pope and share the Eucharist.

Christian Everyone who believes in Jesus, is baptized, and follows the teachings of Jesus.

Consecration The bread and wine become the Body and Blood of Christ through the words and actions of the priest, and the power of the Holy Spirit.

Creed A prayer that says what we believe. At Mass the Nicene Creed is prayed.

Eucharistic Prayer The Church's great prayer of thanksgiving and praise to God.

Gospel The four books of the New Testament that tell the story of Jesus and his teachings. The word gospel means "good news."

grace God's own life within us. The word *grace* means "gift." Grace helps us follow Jesus more closely.

Holy Communion Receiving the Body and Blood of Christ in the Eucharist.

homily A special talk given by the priest at Mass. The homily helps us apply the Word of God to our everyday life.

Lamb of God A prayer said before Communion at Mass. In this prayer Jesus is the Lamb of God. We ask him to take away our sins and make us worthy to receive Holy Communion.

Last Supper The Passover meal Jesus ate with his disciples the night before he died. At the Last Supper, Jesus changed bread and wine into his Body and Blood.

Liturgy of the Eucharist The part of Mass for remembering, giving, thanking, and taking part in the life, death, and Resurrection of Jesus.

Liturgy of the Word The part of Mass during which the Scripture readings, homily, Creed, and Prayer of the Faithful take place.

Lord's Prayer The prayer Jesus taught his followers. It is truly the summary of the whole Gospel. This prayer begins with the words, "Our Father."

Memorial Acclamation A statement of faith after the Consecration at Mass in which we remember the death, Resurrection, and future coming of Christ.

mercy The loving kindness that God shows us.

mission The work or job you are called to do. The mission of the Church is to spread the Word of God.

original sin The sin of the first humans that is passed on to all generations. Human nature was wounded by the first sin and is deprived of original holiness and justice. Original sin also describes the pull everyone feels toward doing things that are wrong.

Passover Jewish feast to remember how God saved the Jewish people from slavery in Egypt and gave them new life. Jesus ate the Passover meal with his friends on the night before he died.

procession Symbolizes moving toward God—moving from our everyday lives and situations into a sacred space and time.

sacrifice A gift to God for the sake of something else. Jesus sacrificed himself on the cross to free us from sin.

Sign of Peace A gesture given to others at Mass that shows we want to be one with them.

Music Lyrics

Psalm 100—We Are God's People

Refrain

Nosotros somos su pueblo.
We are God's people.
Y ovejas de su rebaño.
The flock of the Lord.

1. Make a joyful noise to the Lord, all the Earth.
worship the Lord with gladness;
come in the presence of the Lord with singing.

2. Know that the Lord is God,
our maker to whom we belong.
We are the people of God,
the flock of the Lord.

Somos El Cuerpo De Cristo / We Are the Body of Christ

Refrain

Somos el cuerpo de Cristo.
We are the body of Christ.
Hemos oído el llamado.
We've answered "Yes," to the call of the Lord.
Somos el cuerpo de Cristo.
We are the body of Christ.
Traemos su santo mensaje.
We come to bring the Good News to the world.

1. Cantor: Dios viene al mundo a través de nosotros.
All: Somos el cuerpo de Cristo.
Cantor: God is revealed when we love one another.
All: We are the body of Christ.
Cantor: Al mundo a cumplir la misión de la Iglesia,
All: Somos el cuerpo de Cristo.
Cantor: Bringing the Light of God's mercy to others,
All: We are the body of Christ.

2. Cantor: Cada persona es parte del reino;
All: Somos el cuerpo de Cristo.
Cantor: Putting a stop to all discrimination,
All: We are the body of Christ.
Cantor: Todas las razas que habitan la tierra,
All: Somos el cuerpo de Cristo.
Cantor: All are invited to feast in the banquet.
All: We are the body of Christ.

Hear Our Prayer

Refrain

Hear our prayer, hear our prayer.
Hear our prayer, Lord, hear our prayer.
Hear our prayer.

1. God of the ages,
we look to you to guide all leaders
to seek your truth.
2. God of the suff'ring, hear us, we pray.
Comfort your people, hold us to you.
3. God of the searching, hear us, we pray.
Guide us in safety and lead us home.
4. God of the broken, hear us, we pray.
Nourish our hungers and heal our hearts.

Malo, Malo

Refrain (Cantor intones each phrase, All repeat)

Malo! Malo!	*[Tongan, mah-loh mah-loh]*
Thanks be to God!	
Obrigado! Alleluia!	*[Portuguese, o-bree-ga-doh]*
¡Gracias!	*[Spanish, grah-see-ahs]*
Kam sa ham ni da!	*[Korean, kahm sah hahm nee dah]*
Malo! Malo! Thanks be to God!	

Verses: Cantor; All Repeat

1. Si Yu'us maa'se!	[Chamoru, see joos mah-ah-sih]
Terima kasih!	[Indonesian, three-mah kah-seeh]
Maraming sala mat!	[Tagalog, mah-rah-meeng sah-lah-maht]
Danke schön!	[German, dahn-kuh shuhn]
Dzi kuj!	[Polish, jehn-koo-yeh]
We thank you, Lord!	
2. Mèsi bokou!	[Creole, meh-see boh-koo]
Xie Xie!	[Mandarin, shee-eh shee-eh]
Arigato!	[Japanese, ah-ree-gah-toh]
Grazie!	[Italian, grah-tsee-eh]
Cám n!	[Vietnamese, gahm urn]
We thank you, Lord!	

♪ We Remember

Refrain

We remember how you loved us to your death,
and still we celebrate, for you are here;
and we believe that we will see you
when you come in your glory, Lord.
We remember, we celebrate, we believe.

1. Here, a million wounded souls are yearning just to touch you and be healed.
Gather all your people, and hold them to your heart.

3. Christ, the Father's great "Amen" to all the hopes and dreams of ev'ry heart,
Peace beyond all telling, and freedom from all fear.

4. See the face of Christ revealed in ev'ry person standing by your side,
Gift to one another, and temples of your love.

Words and Music by Marty Haugen

7404 S. Mason Ave., Chicago, IL 60638 • www.giamusic.com • 800.442.1358

♪ Go Make A Difference

Refrain

Go make a diff'rence.
We can make a diff'rence.
Go make a diff'rence in the world.
Go make a diff'rence.
We can make a diff'rence.
Go make a diff'rence in the world.

1. We are the salt of the earth,
called to let the people see
the love of God in you and me.
We are the light of the world,
not to be hidden but be seen.
Go make a diff'rence in the world.

2. We are the hands of Christ
reaching out to those in need,
the face of God for all to see.
We are the spirit of hope;
we are the voice of peace.
Go make a diff'rence in the world.

3. So let your love shine on,
let it shine for all to see.
Go make a diff'rence in the world.
And the spirit of Christ will be with us as we go.
Go make a diff'rence in the world.

Pan de Vida

Refrain

Pan de Vida, cuerpo del Señor,
cup of blessing, blood of Christ the Lord.
At this table the last shall be first, poder es
server, porque Dios es amor.

1. We are the dwelling of God,
fragile and wounded and weak.
We are the body of Christ,
called to be the compassion of God.

2. Ustedes me llaman "Señor,"
me inclino a lavarles los pies:
Hagan lo mismo, humildes,
sirviéndose unos a otros.

3. There is no Jew or Greek,
there is no slave or free;
there is no woman or man;
only heirs of the promise of God.

Amen, El Cuerpo de Cristo

Refrain

Amén. El Cuerpo de Cristo. Amén.
La Sangre del Señor.
Eating your body, drinking your blood,
we become what we receive. Amén. Amén.

1. Amén. We remember your dying and
your rising.
Amén. Y contigo, Señor, resucitamos.
Amén.

2. Amén. Now we offer the sacrifice you
gave us.
Amén. Te ofrecemos, Señor, todo lo que
somos. Amén.

3. Amén. Lord, you make us one body and
one spirit.
Amén. En tu cuerpo, Señor, un pueblo
santo. Amén.

4. Amén. We find you when we serve the
poor and lowly.
Amén. A ti mismo servimos en los po-
bres. Amén.

5. Amén. We look forward to your return
in glory.
Amén. Esperamos el día de tu venida.
Amén.

I Send You Out

Refrain

I send you out on a mission of love.
I send you out on a mission of love.
I send you out on a mission of love,
and know that I am with you always
until the end of the world.

1. I baptize you in the name of the Father.
   I baptize you in the name of the Son.
   I baptize you with the Holy Spirit.
   Go out and spread Good News!

2. Well, it's time for us
   to become people with spirit.
   It's time for us
   to become people of love.
   It's time for us
   to know that Jesus Christ is risen,
   forgives our sins, and brings us new life!

Open Our Ears

Open our ears to your word, Lord.
Open our minds to understand.
Open our hearts to the love of your truth
and to live out your word as best we can.

Words and Music by Darryl Ducote

Let the Children Come

Refrain

Let the children come to me,
let the children come,
Let the children come to me,
Let the children come.

1. What you've hidden from the wise,
   Let the children come.
   You made clear to children's eyes.
   Let the children come.

6. Those who would be first and best,
   Let the children come.
   Must with gladness serve the rest.
   Let the children come.

7. When you welcome one of these,
   Let the children come.
   Be assured, you welcome me.
   Let the children come.

Come to the Table

Refrain

Come to the table of life everlasting, take this bread and be God's presence.
Come to the table of hope for all people, take this cup and live in the love of God.

1. Ev'ry hunger fed, ev'ry thirst is quenched in this bread of new life, wine of our peace: Jesus Christ our Lord!

2. When we eat this bread, when we drink this cup, we share in your death, we share in your life, until you come in glory.

3. Food from heav'n above, living sign of love, come fill our hearts, come fill our minds with faith, hope and love.

Words and Music by Tony Alonso

Gathered As One

Refrain

Gathered as one in Jesus your Son,
lifting our voices in praise,
we know and believe and long to receive
the bread that is strength for our days,
gathered as one!

1. Many faces, the young and the old,
gathered as one in our God!
Throughout hist'ry the story's retold,
gathered as one in our God!
Like those come before us, we listen and learn.
We remember the promise and await your return.
So without hesitation a new generation
proclaims the salvation of God!

3. Many voices, raised up in song,
gathered as one in our God!
In one fam'ly where all can belong,
gathered as one in our God!
Like those come before us, we listen and learn.
We remember the promise and await your return.
So without hesitation a new generation
proclaims the salvation of God!

Pescador de Hombres

1. Tú has venido a la orilla,
no has buscado ni a sabios ni a ricos;
tan sólo quieres que yo te siga.

Estribillo

Señor, me has mirado a los ojos,
sonriendo has dicho mi nombre,
en la arena he dejado mi barca,
junto a ti buscaré otro mar.

Refrain

O Lord, with your eyes set upon me,
gently smiling, you have spoken my name;
all I longed for I have found by the water,
at your side, I will seek other shores.

1. Lord, you have come to the seashore,
neither searching for the rich nor the wise,
desiring only that I should follow.

Agua de Vida

Refrain

Water of Life, holy reminder;
Touching, renewing the body of Christ.
Agua de vida, santo recuerdo;
une y renueva al cuerpo de Cristo.

1. Vengan, reciban el agua de paz,
revivan su santo bautismo.
Dejen atrás los rencores de ayer
y vivan la nueva alianza.

4. All generations, come forth and receive
the blessing of this holy water;
making us one with the God who forgives,
the one who is faithful and just.

5. Bringing new hope to the children of God,
regardless of color story;
cleansing our spirits with kindness and truth,
and keeping the promise alive.

GIA Publications, Inc.
7404 South Mason Avenue
Chicago, IL 60638
(800) 442-1358
(708) 496-3828
www.giamusic.com

OCP Publications
5536 NE Hassalo
Portland, OR 97213
(503) 281-1191
www.ocp.org

World Library Publications
A division of J.S. Paluch Co., Inc.
3708 River Rd. Suite 400
Franklin Park, IL 60131
(800) 566-6150
www.wlpmusic.com
wlpcs@jspaluch.com